FIVE MORE MINUTES

REV. J. W. ARNOLD

For distribution, ordering and contact information, please refer to the last page of this book.

© Copyright 2002 by Rev. J.W. Arnold
ISBN # 0-9740922-4-X

This is the first in a series of books containing articles written by Rev. J.W. Arnold for our weekly Sunday bulletin. They have been a blessing to the Pentecostals Of Gainesville and I trust to the reader, also.

All rights reserved. No part of this book may be reproduced in any form without written permission from Rev. J.W. Arnold.
The Pentecostals Of Gainesville
8105 NW 23rd Avenue
Gainesville, FL 32606
(352) 376-6320
www.gainesvilleupc.net

Five More Minutes

A BookEnds Press Publication
PO Box 14513
Gainesville, FL 32604

IF I BE LIFTED UP

The nation of Israel had been traveling toward their destiny and in the process they began to murmur about the way. God was very angry, sending serpents to bite and judge them. Moses interceded for them and God told him to make a brazen serpent and lift it up on a pole to allow any and all to look upon and be healed. This was a picture of what Jesus would do for our sins when He was lifted up on the cross. He has become the great remedy for our sins. We must look unto him to be spared from the penalty of our sins that is death.

Jesus stated that if He would be lifted up, he would draw ALL MEN unto Him, showing that He bares no animosity toward sinful men. He came to seek and save lost humanity through His dying, resurrection and infilling of the Holy Ghost. His willingness to be lifted up before all as a common criminal, beaten, cursed, humiliated and shamed should be enough to move any person to REPENTANCE. He had no sin. He received our sins, took our place, experienced the treatment due us and all this willingly.

I feel that there should be a different lifting up of Jesus besides the cross of shame, Namely A Life of Godliness. Our lives, our speech, our appearance, our attitudes, our actions should all be avenues that LIFT JESUS UP so that He will draw mankind to Him. What a great responsibility we have to daily lift Him up living in a world that surely does not. May God help us to lift Him up, to praise His name, to sing His song, to seek to show our world that He is Worthy of our all. Let's lift Him up.

LET YOUR LIGHT SO SHINE

God is surely interested in our life styles because they represent Him to a dying world. The Bible states that God has brought us out of darkness into His marvelous light for more than the saving of our souls. He expects our lives to show forth the praises of Him who has done this. A life of praise and purity should be a definite goal for all of the redeemed.

To witness verbally is one thing, but to witness daily with our actions may be quite another. I am sure all of us at times realize we miss grand opportunities to really let the Lord shine in and through us. I want to be saved for sure, but I also desire to allow Jesus to be glorified in my life so that I am not a liability. Are you shining? Are you doing all you can to make Jesus known? When the Pastor asks you to refrain from some things for the sake of your soul and for the sake of the church, do you shine or whine?

Because we all owe such an awesome debt to Jesus for granting salvation to such understanding folks, being willing to shine for His cause should be top priority. To magnify Jesus we must walk in the light, the truth, the way of holiness, the good and right way, or nothing good and lasting can come from our salvation but the mere saving of our own lives. That is not what He intended. Let us look hard and long into our lives being totally honest about every attitude, action, and area. It should be held by every saved person as a high honor to allow our lives to reflect and reveal Jesus. Let us alter any and all areas with zeal as we reflect on how much we owe to His great love.

May God help all of us to use the time we have been allotted to SHINE, SHINE, SHINE...

CREATIVE TROUBLE

Trouble for the most part is always seen in a negative light, something we seemingly dread and wish to avoid. Yet adversity and troubles can be most helpful and productive if we view them properly. First we must believe nothing can come our way without Divine Permission and Purpose. Joseph received terrible treatment from his brothers and others, yet he apparently said this must be for some higher purpose and so instead of crying about it, he poured himself into his situation with vigor and thus the Adverse helped Advance Him into life changing events. Our only control regarding the adverse will be our response to them. Times of trouble can be great revealers about weaknesses within, areas that need to be developed. Faith must be tested if we are to trust it. Let life's adversity be a friend sent to us because our Father loves us rather than a foe sent by our enemy. When we respond properly to problems tho' we see no way out, or blessing from, we disarm our foe and honor our Father.

IF THOU FAINT IN THE DAY OF ADVERSITY, THY STRENGTH IS SMALL. Proverbs 24:10 ADVERSITY BREAKS SOME WHILE IT PROPELS OTHERS TO BREAK RECORDS, BREAK THRU AND BREAK OUT of the average mediocrity of the masses. God grant all of us the vision to view whatever has arrived as adversity and the CUP which OUR FATHER has seen fit to hand to us and not another. Nothing sent from HIM will be able to destroy us, only develop and deliver. Be creative in facing your troubles, there is a way through, around, under and over it. Just search for that way, GOD WILL HELP YOU!!

BE THOU FAITHFUL

Living for the Lord Jesus today at times may seem so hard but His actual requirements have been the same since He first spoke to mankind. BE THOU FAITHFUL is surely within the reach of any and all. Seeing we are called out of darkness, set free by His Great Grace, Forgiven of our terrible past deeds, filled with His lovely Spirit, Blessed by reading His Word and Helped by His Heavenly Host daily. We are promised by Jesus Himself that He would never abandon us. WHAT IS HARD ABOUT STAYING FAITHFUL…seeing He will always do His part. Why do we get so crazy, turned around, upset over things to the point that some among us no longer want to contribute to the health of the body? If I can't be the head, I don't want to be the arm, in fact, I don't want to be involved with helping the health of the body nor will I reach for any others to help them in to the body…VERY STRANGE INDEED.

As a little boy I would get mad if I didn't get to play certain positions on the team or wasn't asked to play. In my stupid way, I would just take the ball and bat home so they couldn't play or if they had a ball and could play, I would go around to the kids and recruit all I could to play my own game. I JUST WASN'T A TEAM PLAYER and I sometimes see that attitude displayed by ADULTS around here. If I can't WHATEVER I'll start my own game or just sit in the seats and criticize the one being played.

We are Stewards of God, of time, money, talents, and opportunity. We are required to be faithful to Him who has placed us in the body. THE CROWN FOLLOWS BEING FAITHFUL.

THE GREAT CHALLENGE

Life all by itself seems to be quite a challenge–bills to pay, kids to raise, finding time to accomplish needful duties, seeking to mature in all areas of life and on and the list goes. Yet the great challenge to all of us is not health or wealth, nor social status, it is internal. Many have tried to truly conquer the world but the real issue is SELF. It is truly the TOUGHEST FRONTIER. Since we have been into self so long, any alterations we seek to do, any subtractions we try to make or any additions we must make, usually are met with FEROCITY and AGITATION.

We spend most of our lives seeking to get into a groove that we and others approve and then along comes THE LORD with HIS WAYS and everything comes tumbling down around our shoulders. He delights in challenging all types of areas in our lives; and, of course, HE is always right and always LORD. His great love for us will not allow things in our lives to stay the same. He has a destiny for each of us and we would do well to bow the HEART to HIS DICTATES quickly. While we usually are vocal and active about various areas OUTSIDE that seek to hinder us, PLACES, PEOPLE AND THINGS, the great battle is still WITHIN the chambers of our hearts.

The Bible states that anyone who can conquer oneself is GREATER than one who is able to win a city. The FOE within is surely the one with which we must reckon and usually the last one to surrender if indeed he EVER does. We must deal with the WEAKNESS WITHIN OUR HEARTS and that surely is a full–time job. May god grant GRACE and HONESTY to accomplish it.

THE POWER OF REAL PURPOSE

Few things in life have the power to alter situations, attitudes or effect God Himself like PURPOSE. The Bible tells of the building of the Tower of Babel with the wrong motive and yet because of the PURPOSE in HEART, God was moved to come down and step into the situation and stop it. Genesis 11:6 states that because of their commitment and purpose (imagined) nothing would be impossible to them. Purpose was so powerful, even Heaven itself took notice and got involved. What would happen in this church if all the BELIEVERS would begin to purpose in their hearts and spirits that GOD WOULD BE FIRST in all areas of life? What power would be released if we would PURPOSE TO PRAY DAILY and FERVENTLY FOR HOLY GHOST REVIVAL NOW…?

Daniel purposed in his heart to not defile himself with the king's meat and God gave him favor and wisdom to affect his situation. We all can look back into our past and see different times that we purposed to do something, or that we purposed to not yield to this or that. The POWER OF PURPOSE gives extra strength to hold on and the courage to go through a tough time. I have had to battle many things much greater than I was, but God granted me PURPOSE OF HEART and it gave me what I needed. Purpose is much more than mental games people play, beyond POSITIVE MENTAL ATTITUDE. It's knowing what is right and holding that course even if you hold to it alone!

Paul's great career was surely a result of his personal PURPOSE regarding the GOSPEL he loved so much. "NONE OF THESE THINGS MOVE ME" he said, regarding sufferings predicted. His PURPOSE–DRIVEN NATURE surely gave birth to his tenacity and sacrifice.

May the Lord grant us PURPOSE OF HEART TO FINISH OUR COURSE AND DO HIS HOLY WILL WITH JOY.

BELONGING OR ACCOMPLISHING

The other day I read a short article about a boy who heard his dad telling someone on the phone that he would be glad to be a part of their group, stating, I already belong to a dozen or so. The boy simply asked his father "Dad, do any of those groups you belong to know that you belong?" Apparently that question affected the Dad so deeply, that the dad quit most of the groups and poured his time and energies into a few specific causes.

It is surely very possible to belong and accomplish little. Do you belong to any groups, causes or even this church that never really receives any real benefit to you belonging? Our day is a generation of joiners and causes. More than emotion and membership is needed if any real good is to be done. Someone must get involved, sacrifice time and money and inconvenience ourselves to accomplish.

Ask yourself right now; do I belong to this assembly and yet it receives very little blessing from my belonging? Is this church any better from my belonging or am I any better for being here?

Achievement does not come easy in any field. Obstacles abound and come in varied shapes and sizes. The lady with the issue of blood had to overcome the greatest obstacle of all. There were people in her path hindering instead of helping. The lame man who came through the roof only did that because people were between him and Jesus.

Maybe it is time to take a long hard look at the barriers in our lives that hinder us from achieving while telling us it is enough to belong. Honesty is always painful but productive if one truly wishes to achieve. Paul told us to examine our own selves to see if we are in the faith, not just belong but achieve anything for the kingdom.

BEYOND THE MOMENT

So many great things happen in out lives in just a moment, yet life is surely much more than a moment. I know we are told to use our time wisely and to do our best while it is called TODAY, but we are greater than this little moment of time. We are ETERNAL BEINGS since we came from God and will return to God. While we are told to provide for our families and live honestly, we are also told to do something regarding our SOULS since that soul keeps living on and on. Jesus said that we profit nothing if we gain the world and then lose our souls. Apparently He saw the WORTH of the SOUL far beyond all material gain. I know how easy it is to get tunnel vision in this matter—working and living yet ignoring the real future facing all mankind.

I read this the other day and wanted to share it with you. "HE WHO PROVIDES FOR THIS LIFE BUT TAKES NO CARE FOR ETERNITY IS WISE FOR A MOMENT BUT A FOOL FOREVER." To win whatever in this thing called TIME and then LOSE in eternity has to be the greatest tragedy in life. We must do something today about our tomorrow, for God has done so much to help make us ready.

I must not ignore the eternal for the moment, for shortly Jesus will come and then our moments will blend into THE EVERLASTING. May God help all of us to use this moment wisely.

'TIS THE SEASON TO BE

That great time of year has once again arrived, with all its songs, parties, gift buying, special desserts, goodies and above all the DANGER OF MISSING THE REASON FOR IT! I hope you will not write me off as some old pain who doesn't like CHRISTMAS. I feel a need to sound a warning during this wonderful holiday season we are now entering.

I do thank God for His coming into this world to do battle with my enemy and for giving His life on Calvary to set me free. My concern is that we will be swept down the river by money mongrels of sales and advertising so that we not only miss the reason for the season, but inadvertently, WE CHEAPEN CHRISTMAS by making it a CELEBRATION of something it was never intended to be. This should be a grand time to reflect how good God has been to all of us. How much we have failed to do in light of His Mercy and Grace and time to set our PRIORITIES afresh.

If this time is the BIRTHDAY BASH FOR JESUS, what are you really planning to give HIM seeing it is HIS GREAT BIRTHDAY PARTY? You would not attend a party in one's honor and then only bring a gift for yourself or worse, someone else who is not the BIRTHDAY CHILD.

I hope you will consider giving something into the WORK OF GOD this season, maybe something grand like more of yourself. I am very glad that God has been good to all of us. I just feel I must warn all of us that it seems very easy to get lost in the COMMERCIALISM and miss THE CHRIST of the CHRISTMAS.

I pray that all of us will take some extra time in the midst of the madness to read the Biblical story again. Take time to reflect on it and the impact it has had in your life. Then give whatever gifts and etc. you wish, with a fresh appreciation for HIS COMING TO THE WORLD.

IT CAME UPON A MIDNIGHT UNCLEAR

That wonderful night so long ago that we are now celebrating was anything but a CLEAR NIGHT SPIRITUALLY. Israel was under Roman rule, religion had become a total sham, faith was very low among many, the economy was poor and the NIGHT WAS VERY DARK. The wonder of it all is that into that mess, HE CAME and still does the same today.

The situation can be a disaster, the condition of the people spiritually may be horrible, but HE COMES ANYWAY. No wonder CHRISTIANITY is so grand, the GOD of all the universe, wills to stoop down into the mess we have made and wills to help any and all. I marvel at HIS GREAT LOVE and GRACE that He is always offering. None are excluded regardless of RACE, CULTURE, CHILDHOOD UPBRINGING or PRESENT CONDITION, the BABE BORN IN THAT BARNYARD STILL REACHES FOR ALL MANKIND. He is called that DAYSTAR FROM ON HIGH, the BRIGHT and MORNING STAR, the dawning of a new day for those who are honest enough to see their need and seek HIM.

It seems that our present day is also anything but CLEAR. Issues are getting clouded, concepts perverted, ideals are being forsaken, beliefs ridiculed, faith seems to be mocked and yet HE IS BEING BORN IN HEARTS EVERYWHERE. All He needs is a little room among the junk that our lives get cluttered with, a MANGER will do for a start. You and I have to make some room for HIS ARRIVAL and then adjust our lives to insure HIS SURVIVAL in our lives. We can starve HIM right out of our lives while we feed our flesh, our emotions and drives. He claims to be the LIGHT OF THE WORLD and that is good news since we are living in an UNCLEAR, UNSURE, UNFRIENDLY, UNHOLY and UNWILLING WORLD. We need a clear beacon to lead us, a guide to direct us and a comforter to aid us, which JESUS IS!

HOW'S YOUR SERVE?

Servanthood seems to be tops on the Lord's list and usually last on man's. Jesus said, "He that would be greatest among you, shall be your servant." So apparently, SERVICE is the road to greatness. It is so easy to let the spirit of this day affect our attitudes and thus be reflected through our actions.

A rider on horseback came across a group of men trying to move a fallen tree from the path, while a well-dressed corporal gave commands to heave. "Why don't you help them?" The rider asked. To which he quickly replied, "I'M THE CORPORAL" Dismounting and laying hold of the fallen tree, he cried, "O.K. fellas, all together now, HEAVE." The tree moved easily with the help of the additional man who told the corporal, "The next time you need some help, send for the chief." It was then the corporal realized the stranger was the COMMANDER-IN-CHIEF, General George Washington.

No person is really too great to help others. In fact, it is only a real small person who refuses to SERVE. God is blessing. Get involved somewhere in this work. Ask what can I do to SERVE the KING: He welcomes all.

THE CHURCH

Jesus said He would build His Church and the gates of hell would not prevail against it. This wonderful statement is so full of rich thought. Let's take a moment with it.

1. The Church is God's idea, His plan, His purchased People and His continuous project through the ages...

2. The Church would be built, not wished into existence, nor beaten into something, but rather built. That requires raw material, (US) a skilled designer builder (JESUS) and considerable time.

3. Hell won't prevail indicates that it would surely try to mess things up. Jesus seems to be saying; a tremendous struggle will occur but HE would see to it that HIS PURCHASED PEOPLE would become HIS PROTECTED AND PERFECTED PROJECT right in the face of the FOE...

From the above thoughts, we should ask ourselves if we are doing all we can for His Church, so we don't find ourselves siding with His Enemy. "He that is not with Me, is against ME," Jesus said, and if the Church is His Purchased Project, we need to help it become all He wants it to be.

Remember, the People who comprise the Church are purchased, His raw material, personally chosen by Jesus. NOT PERFECT, but in a PROCESS of BECOMING. You wouldn't quit or attack your family over imperfections. Why criticize, refuse to work in or worse, why leave the church? JESUS HASN'T, NEITHER SHOULD YOU. LET'S HELP BUILD WHAT HE IS BUILDING.

PROVE YOURSELF

Paul wrote to the Ephesian Church that they should examine themselves to see if they were in the faith. Self searching is often quite an unpleasant task, especially if we are very sincere in our search. To be in the Faith would surely involve a past experience with the Lord, but the challenge is to see if we have made any progress in the journey. Am I growing in my praying and studying? Do I worship any better now? What about bearing fruit? To be in the Faith surely involves going ahead, stepping into new areas of challenge and being willing to change. Stability comes from being attached to certain truths, while Growth must come from change, storms, time and overcoming.

Prove your own selves, Paul said. Don't seek security in opinions, books and others. God is quite willing to help all of us if we are honest enough to be naked before HIM.

David asked for a clean heart, a renewed spirit. Have you ever asked for these items? It shouldn't take failure in some area to get us to cry out for a renewed spirit, just some honest reflection regarding our present state. We can keep ourselves from lots of sorrow and setbacks if we would expose ourselves to the King's Search–light and not try to avoid it because we really don't want to change.

While Salvation is a Personal Miracle, it requires that we personally challenge ourselves. Take our temperature and pulse to see how we are doing. As A Pastor, I can only help so far. I pray for all of you, try my best to have good meals for you and lead you as I'm led, but the rest lies with you.

BEHIND AND BEFORE

Paul wrote a wonderful scripture when he told us to forget those things that are behind and reach forth to those things before us...NO MATTER WHAT A PERSON'S PAST MAY HAVE BEEN, THEIR FUTURE IS SPOTLESS. That is the Great Blessing of the Christian Faith. We don't have to be held hostage by our past. The devil is always trying to bring up our mistakes, both intentional and unintentional. God won't listen to him, and neither should we. If we are willing to confess and forsake our sins God is always ready to cleanse us, wipe the slate clean and let us start afresh.

Thank God for the precious blood of Jesus Christ. I am so glad God has forgiven and forgotten my past. I battle in my mind and emotions with the pages of my past, but that is not God's will for me. Our reach for the before can be so easily hampered by what is behind us. Paul said, "I must forget what is behind and go forward, not dragging yesterday with me as I reach for a fresh something in God." Forgetting actually means refusing to allow them to hold onto you, emotionally destroying you and stopping you from accomplishing what God has intended.

May God grant each of us the faith to apply this truth to our lives, and go forward, knowing that HE who has promised is faithful and True. He wants us to be free from the Prison of the Past.

THOUGHTS ARE POWERFUL

How often have we read or heard, You are what you eat? We are also greatly affected by how we think. Our adversary battles all of us in the mind, for thoughts can become our words or deeds. In fact, thoughts have the power to create dreams of victory or pictures of impending defeat. Israel had lots of promises, God's Presence and powerful problems to deal with. Their thoughts came to them from viewing the problems, without the promises and His Presence.

We must guard our thought–life, for that area has the ability to create both Fear and Faith. We must take deliberate action to ingest the Word (God's Thoughts) and view each episode in life through this FILTER. We must cast down imaginations that say we can't, or how can we? If God has told us, leave the details with Him. Believe Him though your mind, reason and emotions are crying out saying, "YOU MUST BE CRAZY!"

We serve a Faithful Lord, who by the way has never lied, nor lost a battle and who is very pleased with folks who will trust Him when obstacles try to get us to think and act otherwise. May God help each of us to align our thoughts with His and thus defeat our enemy.

COMMITTED

To be committed, says one writer, is "to have a passion, an ultimate loyalty to something you really believe in."

Commitment seems to be the common denominator of greatness, regardless of the field of endeavor. Our lives are not worth much without believing in causes and giving ourselves to them. Contrary to our media agents, life is really not about prosperity, winning and success. It is really about the growth and maturing of our spirit.

Jesus said to win the whole world and lose our souls would be the worst tragedy. No one has ever been more committed to his purpose than Jesus. He gave his all for the accomplishment of his cause and goal. It actually cost him his life, yet he thought we were worth the price. Paul spent his life for the cause of Christ. His sufferings didn't stop him but served in helping him to reexamine them and emerge stronger and greater.

Tough times do help all of us to reevaluate our commitments, define them more clearly and hopefully refuel us to finish the course we have set our sails for. Commitment also serves to identify for us what is really important. The challenge is that commitment does require constant attention. It is so easy to make a commitment and then go into auto-pilot. This is why so many marriages fail. We must feed our commitment, pay attention to and keep realigning our lives to their completion. Commitment must be renewed to survive.

How is your commitment to the Lord? Slipped some? A little cool? May God grant us an honest examination today.

WHERE ART THOU?

These seem to be the first words of God to Adam after his fall from the place of innocence. Like the teachers we had in school, God already knew the answer but he wanted to see if the pupil was aware of the right answer. God has always wanted us to he aware of where exactly we were in various situations. It is extremely important for us, now in the light of his coming, to know just Where Are We? Considering the fate of our eternal souls, it is no laughing matter to be ignorant about the condition of our souls. So much has been provided for us: Calvary, Pentecost, Angels, the Word, the Church, the throne of Grace. We should be concerned about where we really are. Have we grown any since we first were saved? Won any souls in the last year? Have the habits that held us hostage been whipped? Attitudes adjusted? Doing better about PRAYER, TITHES, GIVING, WORSHIPPING, ATTENDANCE, FORGIVENESS?

God's original question was so deep within His heart it caused the INCARNATION. He came looking for his lost sons, wanting us back although we had so badly mistreated him and his grace. He came to seek and save that which was lost. His mission was a Love Journey beyond compare. He is still asking each of us today: WHERE ARE YOU in relationship to MY KINGDOM and its CLAIMS? God surely deserves the best from us and first place in our lives. WHERE ARE WE regarding His will for us?

God grant us the courage to answer his call with naked honesty, for it will affect our soul's destiny.

IF GOD BE GOD, THEN FOLLOW HIM

This statement was made by Elijah on the day he challenged the nation regarding who was really God and that they must finally make their decision. No one can ever really give himself to anything properly unless he is really convinced about the product, idea, or person. Today our world is so mixed up about God. They are such easy prey for the dishonest and the mistaken, let alone the Devil. His job is deception that leads to disaster and finally eternal death. Israel knew better about God, but they had not maintained personal contact with Him, so they lived by the past. Religion became a lifeless segment to them, making them susceptible to false doctrines and practices.

We, too, have been blessed to know the things of God. We must guard against letting our lives be directed by the things of God and not by God Himself. Many things can be the Truth, but without interaction with the God of those Truths they can easily become a substitute for the God from whom they flow. The challenge today is so great and serious, seeing we are surrounded by WINDS OF DOCTRINES, each crying for our attention and allegiance. We must spend time in the Word and in the Prayer Closet if we expect to withstand the onslaught of evil aimed at our souls.

If God is really who He says He is, following Him should be our first desire. It should be no sorrowful task to be His servant, for in His Presence is fullness of Joy. He surely desires, as well as deserves our total surrender and service. For as God, he has no equal. He has been so gracious and kind to all of us. He has been so patient with our repeated mistakes. We should take pleasure in following Him...I DO!

GLORIFY GOD

Every child surely wants to make their parents proud of them, to bring some type of honor and happiness their way. As a child I always wanted my folks to never be ashamed or embarrassed by my antics, although too many times it was another story for sure. My folks tried to instill in my brain certain worthwhile principles, although at the time I didn't think they were so precious or even worth my time.

The Bible tells us very plainly that we should seek to honor God and cause praise to come to Him from our lives. This is surely an AWESOME PRIVILEGE to say the least. To have the honor of being a person that could bring pleasure and praise to the Great God is mind boggling. We who are so weak and inferior to so many other beings (Angels) and yet God has set His love upon us and wants our lives TO BE TO THE PRAISE OF HIS GLORY.

Paul tells us to Glorify God in two areas: in bodies and in spirits, which are the Lords. The inner person must be demonstrated through the outer. Both attitude and appearance seem to count with God. We are His House, Temple, Building and His Body. Therefore, we should act and appear accordingly. Our lips and lives should honor Him. Our actions should bring glory to Him. Our appearance should be a statement about who owns this building. The real issue of TRUE HOLINESS occurs when the HEART and the HOUSE EXPRESS THE SAME THING. Jesus is our finest example. There were no areas of contradiction with Him. May God help all of us to truly seek to GLORIFY GOD IN ALL THINGS.

THE REAL ISSUE

Today, the air seems to be so clouded by numerous voices and opinions regarding the issues of life and what really matters. With the pressure being put on our society to achieve and excel, with students in a rat-race for the job market, with companies assaulting each other's products, confusion can be the order of the day. WHAT'S IT ALL ABOUT ANYWAY?????

The Bible is the answer. Man was made by Almighty God. Man was designed with purpose and possessing a Royal Destiny, deceived into disobedience, then driven out of Eden and God's presence, man has been a mess ever since. But God has been working to return us back to our intended place in his presence and Accomplishing His Pleasure. The real issue is not money, position, winning, or possessing. It is realizing we are more than flesh and bone and more than a being of time. We are SPIRIT beings, thus making us more than lower life forms. We were made in God's image, and God is working to return us to that image with all its grand ramifications (RULING AND REIGNING). God has chosen to work through FAITH and not human reason, thus causing the natural man to become irritated and resistant to His idea.

THE REAL ISSUE is: DO WE BELIEVE GOD? Is HE all HE claims to be? Are we really THAT BAD? Do we need another to CHANGE and SAVE us? Must MAN be BROKEN to be BLESSED? EMPTIED to be FILLED? DIE to LIVE? Confess FAILURE to experience VICTORY? Seek an INVISIBLE GOD to Fill an INVISIBLE SOUL with an INVISIBLE POWER so Man can do VISIBLE THINGS?

OUR BUSINESS IS GOD

The Bible shows us that God has always desired that Man should know Him and enjoy being with Him. Any father knows the joy of his children being happy around him and also how great he feels when they seek to please him in various ways.

John 17:2–3 tells us that to know God and the greatest revelation of God, which is Jesus Christ, has been the desire of God since time began. To know Thee, WOW! What a grand opportunity for humans. To experience the Everlasting God and to actually learn about Him and from Him, has got to be the grandest privilege.

How easy it becomes to get blinded by other issues, events, and activities, which may all be important and beneficial, but not really primary. God desires that we deal with Him, walk with Him, talk with Him, seek to please Him and be hungry for more of Him.

The church is strongest when in pursuit of Him and weakest when she is following other things, no matter how religious they may appear. Christianity is actually bringing God into human life. It corrects errors of attitude and action, restoring the lost image of God into man, allowing God to be first and foremost in our lives. Believing in God and knowing God are miles apart. For one is mental and the other experimental and transforming.

May the Lord inspire each of us to seek God intently, thirsting for Him above all else, yearning to know Him better. From this drive, surely great changes will occur.

LIFT UP YOUR EYES

Vision is surely a grand gift from God and to see SPIRITUALLY is more than a gift. It is a practiced and learned art. Muscles are a natural part of the human body, but to add strength and definition requires more than desire. To accomplish becoming stronger and more fit, one must be diligent and committed to certain practices and pains. To believe in Jesus and to really SEE HIM is not the same thing. Focus is involved in the latter and diligence, determination and willingness to work at it no matter the cost or criticism. Did I say CRITICISM? I surely did and with good reason. To follow hard after Jesus, to try and be all He wants me to be, to abandon the normal roadways of HUMANITY, to behold HIM, will forever meet with CRITICS. This is the price one must pay to be in LOVE WITH HIM. You have eyes first and foremost for Jesus.

Life has a way of clouding our vision. Many times with needful things, honest things, but nevertheless things that can hinder us from attaining SPIRITUAL VISION. True vision will always affect our actions, alter attitudes and cause us to be a little odd or different from the rest. I want to lift my eyes higher, off the monetary and lock them into the eternal. Off the problems and behold the answer. To see HIM IS SURELY TO LOVE HIM for all HE is, has done, and has promised to do soon. May God help all of us to LOOK UNTO JESUS for this vision will result in victory.

SIGN HERE PLEASE

I read something this past week that kind of stunned me and then challenged me to do a better job with this thing called LIFE. "EVERY JOB IS A SELF PORTRAIT OF THE PERSON WHO DOES IT." "Autograph your work with excellence," the writer continued. Now that was quite a mouthful. I began to think about all the jobs I have done, am doing and hope to do shortly. What kind of picture have I really drawn with my efforts–a MASTERPIECE or MESSTERPIECE? Did I just get the job done, or did I pour into the effort my best? Sometimes our attitudes surely come through as we are forced to work at situations less than desirable, don't they?

As I reflected on this statement, I wondered how many times various things were done through being irritated and the irritation signed the job and not any type of excellence. Sometimes I wish I could go back and preach a certain message over again with a better spirit and drive but that is not possible I guess. Does anyone wish right now, as you review some of your past deeds, that you would have signed your work with a deeper dedication, sincerity or sacrifice?

I think we all love to read and hear the stories of Jesus in every type of situation and watch Him just shine through in such beauty and charm. He surely signed His work with TRUE EXCELLENCE. I still desire to be like Him. I know He is with me and He also desires that all of us be great epistles for HIS GLORY. As you look at various jobs facing you, consider this little line: EVERY JOB IS A SELF PORTRAIT. SIGN EACH WORK OF YOURS WITH EXCELLENCE. This sure seems easier said than done but by HIS GRACE it can and will be done.

BE NOT WEARY...BUT I AM

Paul told the Galatian folks not to be weary in well doing and that we would reap if we refused to FAINT. Easier said than done. Today finds me very weary with lots of things. I don't feel like I am about to FAINT, but rather I want to FIGHT. Life has a way of wearing one down, especially if one really is trying to PLEASE GOD and help to further HIS KINGDOM. That, of course, will always involve PEOPLE and there is where the irritation, disappointments and hurts seem to flow into our lives.

To really pour oneself out and then seemingly go unheard, or disregarded, sometimes can wear one down. To ask folks please don't do that, please stop wearing that sort of apparel, please stop acting that way, please be more faithful to church services.

To study and pray for real Holy Ghost direction that will help the family of GOD and then to watch your efforts for the most part go unheeded and scorned can be cause for weariness. Maybe that is why Paul wrote that. From being in the work for a long time and knowing the feeling of being frustrated, he wanted the rest of his folks DOWN LINE to rise above it, live through it, and above all, DO NOT FAINT. To faint is like stopping, no further efforts being made, and then OUR ADVERSARY WINS and that just will not do. Weary of pressure, yes! Bills, yes! Temptation, yes! Being hurt, yes! Struggles, yes! Disagreements, yes! Dry spells, yes! And many others. But FAINTING, QUITTING, LEAVING, BEING DISLOYAL TO THE BODY AND GOD: NEVER!

We have come too far now, seen too much, been blessed beyond counting, so I'll just see you at the FINISH LINE, O.K.?

HOW MUCH OWEST THOU MY LORD?

The above statement comes from the teaching in the Bible regarding a steward being called into accountability for his past actions.

In this scene it is quite obvious that every believer shall give an account to the Lord for our time, talents and giftings. We have been bought with a great price, the BLOOD of JESUS, and that alone is enough to cause us to be very committed to our task. The problem is compounded greatly by the fact that the Lord has blessed all of us with untold blessings and acts of kindness beyond any doubt. I am a debtor to HIS GRACE and will be held totally responsible for the USE or MISUSE or even the NONUSE of what He has given to me for the accomplishment of HIS WORK. No one at any time can say they have not been granted the means to do the task. The Lord doesn't save any souls and then send them into the battle UNARMED and WITHOUT RESOURCE. I am sure at times we may feel we are not able, or equipped properly, to be effective in the area we find ourselves thrust into, but it simply is not true. GOD FEEDS WHERE HE LEADS AND SUPPLIES WHERE HE SENDS. Our God is too wise and too wonderful to expect anyone who serves Him to do that service with our own ability.

Considering how much God has done for each of us: pulling us out of our mess, granting total forgiveness, filling us with His Spirit, granting fresh help for repeated mistakes, and constant encouragement, how could any of us feel we OWE JESUS NOTHING, or LIFE'S LEFTOVERS? May God help each one of us today to take a trip hack into our lives and take inventory of HIS GOODNESS TO US and make a fresh effort to do our very best to see HIS WORK DONE WELL.

DIVISION INVITES DISASTER

All through the scriptures, the topic of real unity and agreement seems to be paramount. Over and over the WORD admonishes the family of God to be in agreement with the Lord and with fellow believers. Apparently DIVISION and DISCORD is so disgusting to the Lord maybe because all the conflict and sorrow found in this world is directly related to this very thing –DIVISION.

God suffered a great upheaval in the heavens with Lucifer wanting the praise due God and apparently led a charge against the Throne and was cast out and cast down. The next scene was the GARDEN in which this fallen angel convinced the occupants that they needed to override the restraints God had required. The results were the same, driven out of their home and from the FACE of their FATHER and FRIEND. Tranquillity and Peace are the off spring of AGREEMENT while frustration, upheaval and bitterness flow from a DIVIDED HEART and MIND.

Jesus told us that a divided house cannot stand, even to the point that Satan's own kingdom cannot survive any type of division. Now that is amazing! Jesus said that not one devil will ever try and cast out another one, that they never fight against themselves, nor do they steal from each other. They are totally in unison regarding their purposes. I sure do wish the CHURCH could learn a lesson from these fallen ones. If they won't allow any divisions among themselves, how foolish are we to.

I know that things take place that can cause disagreement but never to the point that we allow divisions and discord so that the work of God must suffer while the ranks of His Army fuss over stuff? May God help all of us to work together for the common good of all.

POWER AND PASSION ARE PARTNERS

How often do we yearn for Old–time Power and yet seem never to taste it nor even come close to it. WHY? I think one reason could be our lack of PASSION WITH REGARD TO TRUTH. The early church had such a devout drive in them which seemed to come from a PASSION about and for the TRUTH. Having been kicked out of their former fellowships over the TRUTH they now embraced, some type of PASSION seemed to PULSATE deep within them which gave a great release of POWER to accomplish the WILL OF GOD. We are debtors to previous generations that suffered for the TRUTH. We cannot drag the banner in the dirt nor let the flame die just because our generation has decided that DOCTRINE and DISCIPLINE have no place in the believer's life. The TRUTH has great power to resist the attack of evil which usually takes the form of INTIMIDATION. TRUTH has the power to set humanity free to become all GOD intended, but TRUTH must be embraced and loved with a PASSION.

I am not talking about being ruthless or unkind towards people, but rather being totally unbending and intolerant towards ERROR in DOCTRINE or LIFESTYLE. Love is the greatest power in the universe. For GOD is LOVE and God is also TRUTH. Jesus told us that in KNOWING the TRUTH we would be set free. Not believing, but knowing, experiencing and embracing personally. The TRUTH was the PERSON of GOD before it became a STATED PRINCIPLE. TRUTH is EVERLASTING and UNCHANGING. We need to ask the LORD to renew within us a fresh fervor for HIS TRUTH, HIS PERSON, HIS PURPOSE and HIS PLAN. The POWER WILL COME FROM OUR PASSION FOR THE TRUTH.

BE AN EXAMPLE TO OTHERS

In the Book of Acts, Peter tells us that Jesus went about doing GOOD, for God was with HIM. It seems that His constant outlook was I MUST GLORIFY MY FATHER with MY ACTIONS. I know that I personally have missed many opportunities to do good, simply because of various distractions, personal agendas and sometimes just plain INSENSITIVITY. JESUS began HIS day with prayer; can we ignore His example and yet expect to have good results? JESUS was so intensely focused about what was important and how precious HIS allotment of time was, nothing could be wasted or misused. HE did good to all sorts of people, treated all types of people with dignity and worth, He hated SIN, yet LOVED SINNERS. HE hated all types of fakery, religious sham, dishonesty in any form, yet was so willing to show great patience and mercy with many failing folks.

He left us so many examples about our behavior, attitudes and outlooks, sometimes I am overwhelmed with how far I seem to be from them. Yet I know HE loves us FREELY and FULLY, and seeks often to help me get my priorities in line with HIS PURPOSES. I know HE wants all of us to EXAMPLE HIS WAYS to our society; showing kindness, compassion and goodness to ALL PEOPLE. To live out the JESUS WAY surely seems so different and difficult, maybe because we have our own brand of concepts we try to operate by.

One thing about being an example, you must go it alone at the start but we are doing it UNTO THE LORD that HE receives the praise. May God grant all of us the DESIRE and GRACE to step out of the parade and do from the heart what HE wants us to do: EXAMPLE HIS WORDS and WILL. The results will be worth It.

DAMAGE CONTROL

The world we live in constantly plays the game of damage control. Not for the sake of the nations good but rather for the protection of the IMAGE. How sad it is that HONESTY does not ever enter the calculations of various groups, especially POLITICAL PARTIES. Any incident that might affect PUBLIC OPINION or could create less than the desired results, is usually buried or is in some way made to appear what it is not.

God also gets involved with DAMAGE CONTROL, but for different reasons and results. To cover up anything with LIES only adds to the mess. God seeks to cover all things with LOVE. He seeks to get us to be convicted and thus confess so HE can be released to forgive us and continue to fellowship. God practices DEVIL CONTROL which sure helps the believer to accomplish the PURPOSE God desires for HIS CHILDREN.

I am very thankful for His constant concern and compassion for my own life. So many times I have been in need of MERCY and PARDON. If I wasn't sure I could find these in God, I surely would be in trouble. I think we should try our best to be more interested in protecting HIS IMAGE and CAUSE than ours. God has often revealed the various FLAWS and FAILINGS of HIS servants, which HOLLYWOOD and POLITICS would never do. HIS WAYS are surely NOT OUR WAYS.

The BELIEVERS mistakes do not seem to grind on the Lord nor do they have the power to separate us from HIS LOVE and PURPOSES. He knows we are CLAY and seeks to transform and conform us regardless of our repeated errors.

The word says love covers a multitude of sins. Apparently, showing the desire of true love is COVERING ANY CASUALTIES and thus CONTROLLING DAMAGE the DEVIL delights in. May God grant all of us a pure heart that seeks to cover rather than to expose. Not because we don't want our image messed with but rather that the DEVIL DOESN'T GET THE ADVANTAGE.

GOD WILL MAKE A WAY WHEN THERE IS NO WAY

We often sing these words during our service times but I wonder if we realize what is really involved for this to happen. In order for the Lord to make a way when none seems to exist, means that we have been allowed by His Power to get into something we cannot get out of, or through, without a miracle. We do believe in miracles but often overlook the soil which is usually required to have them, which simply stated is: THE IMPOSSIBLE. God, who loves us beyond any understanding within us, seeks to send us into trapped situations, blocked on all sides and bank books empty, so that we will change our direction of focus from us to HIM.

We all know the story of Israel at the Red Sea, trapped and being chased. It surely was looking bad for them but God had arranged the situation from start to grand finish. He is the One who loves to deliver and demonstrate how much He cares and controls all things.

I am quite sure those trapped at the sea that day were not really thrilled and checking their theology, but were scared and somewhat upset at their leader. Sound familiar? I thank God for His leading even when I am so confounded and blind to the why and what of the situation. I am so glad God doesn't change His work because we can't seem to believe at the time of pressure, how it will work out or why it has to be this way. God has His ways which are surely past finding out but surely not past experiencing.

Faithful is He who has called us, begun a great work in all of us and too great in Himself to fail or quit. Amen. The Lord Reigneth, Let the Earth Rejoice.

THE POWER OF PERCEPTION– PRO OR CON

How we perceive various situations, people, or life itself, can really determine how we end up–defeated or victorious. The situation may not have the ability to stop us but if we perceive it as impossible, then our perception of the problem is given power it never had.

When Israel spied out the land, the problems regarding the giants and the walled cities were very real but surely not impossible until they perceived them as such. The wrong view of them caused fear to arise within most of them which allowed something to become a barrier that they felt they could not defeat. I know the problems were no match for God but when we perceive anything without including His presence and power, we sentence ourselves to failure and actually insult God with our limited viewpoints.

Problems, setbacks and obstacles are only platforms for God to reveal Himself in a much greater way than before. Nothing can catch Him unaware. Before the problem he had the provision tucked away in the bush just like the ram was waiting in the thicket for Abraham on the mount. I believe He seems to enjoy when we get pinned against the wall in some type of problem, so He can use it to magnify HIS GRACE and show us how much He cares and can do.

Our recent situation regarding the new church building is nothing to HIM, so we must not allow it to become a barrier to us. For with God, ALL things are possible and He knows the end from the beginning. Keep believing and working to have a personal revival and God will come through: For The Lord Reigneth…

PRAISE TO GOD
OR THE PRAISE OF GOD

Peter tells us that God has called us out of darkness that we might show forth the praises of God. Not just to offer vocal noises, but rather that our lives should be a Praise to God. Many times I have heard this verse used to show our need to Praise God vocally and rightly so with Hebrews 13, the fruit of our lips, but one's life can Praise God much greater than one's lips. Truth known can be a great blessing but truth practiced can impact lives for God in a better and greater way. Paul told us that we are epistles seen and read of all men, even though these men may never attend our church services, nor ever hear us sing, shout or praise God vocally. Our best opportunity to magnify God must come through situations where pressure and problems abound, for then the real us seems so obvious.

One writer told us that after we have been saved, our lives should be to the glory of His grace and we must manifest Him to the unchurched world we live in. I must tell you that this challenge is no small task and without the Holy Ghost operating within our lives it shall remain totally beyond our reach and realization. We must have the touch of the Lord on us if we are to affect our society, for it does not need to hear another sermon, it needs to see a sermon lived out under conditions that require the supernatural.

May God grant us the desire and determination to be that sermon lived out before them so that we become a praise to God and not just a praiser of God. I know we all can do better in this area, so let us ask His help to be a praise to Him.

I SAT WHERE THEY SAT

These wonderful words come to us from the Prophet Ezekiel when they were in captivity and his congregation was a company of exiles, captives, beaten and broken people. I don't think any preacher ever had such a group of folks in his congregation like this man, for they had been defeated, humiliated, taken prisoner and carried away to a foreign land to be dealt with as slaves and really non–persons. This prophet tells us the secret of his work among the hurting and defeated: I SAT WHERE THEY SAT and this helped me to understand their heartaches and problems. Rather than preaching to them, I TASTED THEIR TRAGEDIES and this allowed me to become more compassionate and affective.

How long has it been since any of us put ourselves into the other person's pain, their pressure, failures, hurts or whatever? This would surely birth in all of us much greater kindness, concern and tolerance if we would enter into their situations from their viewpoint. I think that we are often out of sympathy with the sick because we are well, the poor because we have enough, the young because we have grown a little older and now we dream and desire much less than when we were their age,

How does the prisoner look out at life? The social outcast? The young girl who chose poorly? The untrained who fights for a job? The minority who must deal with bias and resistance? The sinful, because we have experienced mercy and grace? The lonely, because we have many friends.

Jesus mixed among all sorts to enter into their pains and problems, Shall His saved friends and family keep a safe distance and never try to sit where they now must sit?

Let us make some changes and I am sure we can be more like our Lord Jesus who was touched with people's problems.

THE DESIRE FOR
THE FORMER TIMES

In the book of Job, 29:2, we find him saying, "Oh that I were as in months past." What we might call the backward look, the longing for our yesterdays. Another writer in the Bible tells us that we do not inquire or desire wisely when we say that the former times and days were better than our present. All of us seem to glance over our shoulders at times and wish for what was, the distance of yesterday seems to hold a charm which they didn't have at the time of the episodes. What seemed to be somewhat trashy then seems to have changed into treasure with the passing of time: or are we being deceived?

There are yearnings within all of us for what used to be that I feel are true and right. Things we now miss, people we used to be friends with, jobs we had or some type of security we once had that we now long for. Various situations have now backfired on us, time has been wasted, money has been spent that was hard to come by and we wish that we still had this or that or them. I too must deal with these backward longings, but God is just as great and kind now as He has ever been, just as willing to show us the way now. We must leave the past and move into our futures.

Yesterday seems to hold a safety we now are missing. Feeling a little uncomfortable, we tend to see the past as the greatest when the future from God surely will be much greater than yesterday. I would like to go back and repeat some things. I wish I could talk again to some in a better tone of voice. I wish I had been wiser in some matters, but this cannot happen. I must deal with the harvest of yesterday, knowing God is Greater than my failures and has a great tomorrow planned. Forgetting those things which are behind, I press ahead to the things awaiting me.

LET GOD ARISE AND HIS ENEMIES BE SCATTERED

As we enter this new year, full of hopes, untried waters, enemies lurking in many places, let us seek the face of the Lord that He might be pleased to become very much involved with this assembly. I know He has been so kind and gracious to all of us but I feel very deeply that it is HIS WILL and DESIRE to show HIMSELF STRONGER and GREATER in these last days. I know He has been with us, but not to the degree that He could be, or would be, if we would seek to do HIS WORK as never before. I am very hungry for HIS POWER, PRESENCE and TRUTH to be manifested among us as never before. We say we believe in the supernatural but we see very little of it operating among us to the level we should.

This great gospel we preach should be confirmed with signs and wonders both in the physical and spiritual arena. Anyone receiving the Holy Ghost is a living miracle, and for this we should be very glad but I feel we need to experience HIS POWER in the area of healing and deliverance. Many people today are held hostage by spirits and these take the form of habits and practices that are not pleasing to God nor helpful to the people who practice them. God desires that HIS CHURCH continue the WORK OF JESUS in all areas that HE had done. I know we are not JESUS, but the word says: "Jesus began to do and teach, until He was taken up to heaven." The book of Acts shows that JESUS worked with HIS CHURCH, doing what He had been doing before. Can we do any less?

We must seek God to reveal what we are missing, or doing incorrectly, and allow HIM to work through us. Let God Arise.

THE TRUTH WILL FREE THOSE WHO PAY

Our world has become one giant prison of people who want to be free from many things but unwilling to pay the price for that freedom. Anyone who has ever taken time to study the history of the world knows that freedom is very expensive, but not to pay the price for it is really much more costly. To know the truth, like Jesus told the Jews, meant a lot more than believing something or holding onto a concept or idea. It really meant to embrace that truth until you are now in the process of becoming like the truth you have embraced.

There is no room for arm chair believers who study things and do not apply them to their life: unpracticed truth is no better than error. Truth only liberates those who come to love that truth to such a level they allow it to impact and alter their lives, thus they taste true liberty. Today, many feel If something is required or demanded, it must be legalism or bondage, but the opposite is the real truth.

Jesus came to set the captives free, not initially, but continually until there is not one area in our lives dominated by evil. I have not met anyone to date that had reached this point but I have met many with areas purified and empowered. Honesty is always required for progress with God. This should be easy and God is easy to be around even though we fail often. I want to pay the price for the freedom of my spirit that I can become an asset and not a liability, DON'T YOU?

We must come clean to become clean.

THE MEASURE OF YOUR STRENGTH

Proverbs 24:10 states that if any will faint in the time of adversity, the strength of that person is small. Which means the storm shows or reveals our real strength. Only adversity can reveal just how weak or strong any person is, for anyone can hold the helm when the sea is totally calm. The raging of the sea and blowing of the wind are the things that test our strength and willingness to hold fast to our course. No one really enjoys the adverse, yet God allows various situations to arrive that we might see how weak we are and how much we really need His hand to steady us.

Revelations about ourselves are very painful, yet so needful, and untested faith can't really be trusted. The furnace of affliction seems to be the favorite testing place of the Lord. He knows what it will require to purify and empower each one of us.

Testing and trials are His avenues to improve and enrich each of His children, but we must remember; the hand that deals with us has nail prints in it. Love orders our episodes, not hate or indifference. I do not enjoy the things I am forced to deal with, but when I grasp that God has no intention of me being destroyed by them, I can breathe a little easier.

May God grant us the faith and trust we need to taste the terrible, tragic and troubles that will Honor Him and mature us while defeating the Devil. Help us, Oh Lord.

ALL THINGS ARE POSSIBLE WITH GOD

The Word of God is really His thoughts regarding various areas of our lives, the way He wants us to live, things He wishes for us to experience. The blessings that will come our way if we seek to live in compliance to His wishes. God never has intended us to live on, blind or deaf with regard to what He wants to do and will do. The power that created the universe was the word of God. The breath of God caused matter to take form, life to occur and history to begin. God still has all the power, wisdom, greatness, goodness, life, knowledge, He ever had. He changeth not!

The record of His works in the past now form the platform for our faith to act and expand to new levels. God wills many things within himself that apparently do not always happen to us, and for us, only because of our unbelief. We read various events in the past and say amen, but to believe that they can and will happen to us and our situations, well that is quite another story. The battle is within our very selves. Can we grasp that God wills to do it again? Can we believe this time He wants to use us as the vehicles of His expression? Paul tells us that we have this treasure in earthen vessels that the excellency might be of God and not the containers.

We all battle over ourselves, our faults, failures, frailty, lack of perfection, but the contents will always be able to do more than the container. The container must not stop the flow from within, because the vessel seems too unworthy.

Let God work in and through you, believing He knows how to get the job done the best way and knows all about We Vessels.

THE POWER AND PURPOSE OF THE STORM

Storms are a part of every life, and for the most part they are the defining part of our lives and the revealers of the vessels. Nothing has the power to show what we are made of, or not made of, like the storm. Ships are made to sail and also prevail in a storm, for the ship must be able to overcome what has the power and intent of destroying the vessel. The ship must be made with that intent; enduring storms, attacks and various elements that test the strength of its very character.

Our lives must also face all sorts of winds blowing, waters beating against, the burning sun of temptation challenging the depth of our dedication. The Lord doesn't allow any storm into our lives with some malice of purpose, but rather that we might become aware how much we need His help and how easily life can sweep us away. At best we are very frail creatures, and life does have some powers we are not able to whip by ourselves. The storm is a revealer of our lack of strength and His faithfulness.

All of us could start our talks with the words, "If it had not been for the Lord." Yet God only allows things that will help us grow, confess, seek His help, deliver us from pride and teach us new ways to overcome. Storms can be very scary and long but they will not destroy us if we will keep seeking the Lord and His will, for He is not willing that we worry to death nor get worn slap out.

In our storms, the darkness increases, causing less vision, so we need to know what we believe before we enter it and we won't get off course and lose our way. I know the wind is howling, rain falling, thunder is rolling, but God is in control for all the elements are His anyway.

MY WEAKNESS CAN'T MATCH MY HELPER

All along life's travels, we are confronted with problems within and without that seem so great we are often tempted to despair. It is at those times we must lift our eyes unto the hills from whence cometh our help, our help comes from the Lord who made the heavens and the earth. It becomes impossible for anyone to stay depressed, discouraged, or defeated when that person begins to remember how great their ally is.

All powerful. Almighty. All things possible with God. These terms seem to pulsate with encouragement and hope. My weakness, while being at times very annoying, may also become a platform for His power to be revealed. It seems all through the word God shows His power via the weakness of His people again and again. He delights in delivering us when we cannot. I still seek to be better and fail less, yet I am made to know that I am not loved less because of my various mistakes and repeated blunders. Every devil seems to enjoy attacking each of us in the areas we seem so pitiful about, yet when we refer these pests of the spirit world to our Father, they are not so bold. Ha! Ha!

May each one of us constantly lift our eyes, hearts and faith upward to Him who is able to do more than we can even think or ask. Great Is the Lord.

WATCHMAN, WHAT OF THE NIGHT?

The main job of the watchman was to be a lookout for enemy activity, to help the people become aware of any impending danger. If the watchman didn't do his job, the rest of the city would be greatly endangered and the guilt would fall on that watchman. I feel that God has put we PASTORS in that place of advantage, high up on the wall, that through His Great Grace, we might be able to warn the church regarding enemy activity and help the bride to be ready for Jesus' soon coming. I do not want to spend my life as some negative alarmist, but I must fulfill my job or be found unworthy and unfaithful by the one who appointed me. We are surely living in dark times and we are heading toward the great sunrise of eternal bliss so it behooves us to give heed to the watchman.

I want to be ready for His appearing no matter what the cost, even to the point of being made fun of by many, or isolated by some. To miss the rapture will be the worst nightmare we would ever live in. Examine your lives, check your motives, be careful about your priorities, give your best to the work of God, for God will not forget any labor of love done for His people or church.

Please check into your own prayer lives. Are we praying often? Intensely? Are we ready for His appearing? We must not allow the enemy to lull us to sleep, involve us with material things, cause us not to care about the lost. Shake ourselves, for our Lord draws near, sunrise approaches quickly. It is time to rededicate our lives to our Lord for He wants all of us, not just a part.

Yours From On The Wall.

THE REAL BLESSING OF THE BAD NEWS

No one usually delights or even desires to receive what is called BAD NEWS, for we are all forced all too often to deal with various ugly situations. All of mankind hopes for the best, looks for some type of break, some good report to help us through the tough times. Yet, receiving BAD NEWS at various times can be a blessing of untold proportions. Being told we have some type of sickness can lead us to doing something about it. Hearing some noise under the hood of the car can lead us to an investigation that can save costly repairs. BAD NEWS can help get our attention and, with a proper response, help us to experience a better conclusion.

In the spirit world, we are always confronted with the BAD NEWS FIRST. If not, we would not even think about seeking to change one bit. We must be confronted with, "all have sinned and come short," "there are no righteous persons," "unless we repent we shall all perish," "God is angry with the wicked every day," "you must be born again or you cannot see or enter the kingdom." None of these make us feel good, they are sent to get our attention and cause us to become aware of our desperate situation and turn to God for mercy and help.

The good news about the bad news is that the bad news is not the final news, God has some good news that follows the bad news. He loves us so much He has made a way for us. He wants us to come to Him, so He grants repentance. He wants to live inside each of us, so He has offered the Holy Ghost to all willing to obey him and seek him. God is so great that any news from Him will surely help us.

HEREBY WE PERCEIVE THE LOVE OF GOD

The story of the Cross of Calvary has never lost the grand power of love to this day. FOR GOD SO LOVED, HE GAVE. These are words full of principle for living, namely love must always act towards the object of its love. It cannot stay uninvolved. It has to get working for the good of the one loved. When Jesus went to the cross, it was not a tragedy but rather a triumph of the plan, purpose and love of God. For it had been in the mind and heart of God before the first sin ever disgraced the planet.

To think that a Holy God would come to this little spinning mud ball and walk among us, teach us the best way to live, heal our sick, feed our hungry, set the captives free, bear our sins on the cross, arise from the dead, send back the fire of the Holy Ghost to dwell within us, is beyond my grasp. God so loved me! What an awesome statement. A God who needs nothing still wants me to be part of His family. It has to be divine, because man could not come up with such a plan. Every person has been called by that cross to come look a little closer to see that man on the center tree. He is bearing our sins freely, not forced. I owe that drama my very best, I must use this gift called life to HONOR THE MAN ON THE TREE CALLED JESUS.

May God help each of us to really perceive the Love of God for each of us. We owed a debt we could never have paid, but Jesus picked up the tab. WOW!

WHEN HE HAS TRIED ME AND NOT THE TRIAL

Job has long been a friend to many of us, but I wonder if we really have grasped the full impact of what he really said so long ago. We all know about the terrible trials he endured, but I think we may have missed the key to his victory. Job believed his situation came by permission from His God, for he said, "when He has tried me." Not the trial itself, but His God who ordained it. I feel much better about facing distasteful episodes when I know that My God has been the one who actually handed it to me. If I can be sure within my heart this is God, and not the results of some ignorance on my part, I can live with it better. When Jesus was about to die for us, He spoke of his coming, suffering, mistreatment and death this way; "the cup that my father giveth me." You can see that the trial was not the issue but rather the Hand that gave the cup to him.

When we are sure the trial, test, or whatever, has been personally handed to us from the great hand of love and grace, we can surely deal with it and Honor God by responding in a proper way. I cannot say that I understand, or even appreciate, the various things that I have been handed of late, but I know that God has trusted me with this trial which is something to be happy about; for He does not allow all to be tested severely. I think that God wished for all His kids to be put through various things, but sometimes we are so shallow, self-centered or just plain weak, He knows we will fold or fall so we are then left to stay immature and weak.

May God help us to be counted worthy of whatever testing and trials needful to our growth and transformation. I dislike the problems but I LOVE AND TRUST HIS HAND.

BE READY FOR THAT GREAT DAY

All the world seems to be sensing that something is about to occur, an event or series of events that will either affect or totally alter life on this planet. There seems to be something in the air, an anticipation that is deep within our souls. To the believer that event will be the coming of the Lord for His bride, the catching away known as the rapture. We are so close to that great day it is really terrifying. All our lives we have heard about Jesus and His coming again and now we seem to be the very generation that will see Jesus coming for His church. I know that I do not want to miss it, nor to be playing church games and be lost forever. Jesus warned us in the Bible about being so involved with life and thus missing His Coming. Too many verses warn us not to let that day catch us unaware.

We must begin anew to examine our walk with God. We need to start asking ourselves some pointed and probing questions for our eternal destiny is at stake.

- Do I love God with all of my heart?
- Am I excited about His return?
- Do I really have the Holy Ghost?
- Do I have any unconfessed sin?
- Do I care about the lost?
- Am I doing anything to help the work?
- Is the kingdom a priority with me?
- Am I faithful in finance, time and prayer?

May God help us to be ready for that great day, that is what we have lived, dedicated, self–denying lives for.

IF GOD BE FOR US, WHO CAN BE AGAINST US

We all believe that nothing can stop us from doing the will of God if God himself is really with us. The part that often seems to trip us up is that little word IF. When I am sure of something, I tend to be very bold, even challenging to whatever I am being forced to face or deal with. When I am less than sure about a situation, I tend to be less aggressive and assured. That little IF makes a big difference in so many areas.

How many times have we all wondered about whether God was in this or that, or if we were going in the right direction about something. I have listened to many people about various things and that little IF seemed to be the oft repeated key word: IF I just knew for sure this was HIS WILL, IF I could just hear God say, IF I could only stop doing this or that, IF my mate would only, IF the Bible were clearer about this question, and the list seems to go on and on.

We do not have to doubt about whether God is for us, of course He is, and will be. The incarnation, the shed blood of Jesus, the outpouring of the spirit, the written word of God, the visitation of His spirit all seem to shout GOD IS FOR ME. At all times and in all situations and nothing should shake us loose from this position. We are all just humans and we tend to be more negative than we should. The bad reports seem to be real mountains of impossibility but the real truth is GOD IS FOR US and that puts the favor in our lives for victory.

As we all face the situations of life, may we recall and believe the great truth that GOD IS ON MY SIDE and I AM A WINNER though I must fight to finish.

THE BEST IS YET TO COME

I have been reading the book of Job and the treasures found within that little book are amazing. It is recorded in the last chapter this grand statement; The Lord blessed the latter end of Job more than the beginning–He gave Job twice as much. Most of us would sure welcome the end of Job's story if we could escape the long painful process he went through to get God to bless him double. I know the Lord is still the same. He will not change, and for that I am so grateful. This truth gives me hope that I have not seen all that God may do for me, nor can any situation I must deal with be the final chapter in my life. God is supreme in all things and if He allows loss, pain, setbacks, failures, disappointments and etc., He is able to grant greater things in the future. What devastates us doesn't in any way worry our Lord. He owns the entire earth. All rulers reign by His permission and the devil is on a strong chain and God is holding the other end. Praise God!

We must not make the mistake of measuring tomorrow by the past. For the past has not ever seen all that God can and will do. He has everything under control except our bad responses. Those reactions sometimes are the thieves that steal from us what He wants to grant us. I know Job had lots of bad feelings, outbursts, anguish untold and yet God called him MY SERVANT, JOB. God didn't cast him off even though he was incorrect in a lot of conclusions. Let us believe that God has some great things ahead for us and that nothing can separate us from the love of God.

THE POISON IN PENTECOST— MEDIOCRITY

No one would seek to buy a book called how to be below average, or how I achieved mediocrity, or how to live below your best. No one would go to hear a lecture on coasting through life or doing as little as you can for your company, family or GOD. I feel like we could all use a wake up call regarding mediocrity. The dirty little word that can rob all of us of doing our best. I don't want the Lord to challenge me with a question like "Why didn't you do all you could for me, with all your might?" We are told to work for God with all our strength and to work heartily for our wonderful Lord. Are we doing that or just doing enough to ease our minds and to be acceptable to other mediocre folks that seem to strive for excellence in their field of labor but not in the church.

Seeing that the church is the agency that God has chosen to work through and for, it would seem to me that all of us should be putting the work of the church ahead of any other tasks. If we are heading to the place of accounting, we really should shake our very beings and stop settling for being just average or mediocre. We are debtors to grace and mercy, which should provoke us to striving for being the best we could ever be in His Kingdom. I know we are facing the coming of the Lord and our work for Him carries such potential for reward and our own fulfillment.

Remember; achievers are not just born that way, they are made.

May God help each of us to seek to excel far beyond where we find ourselves today. ATTACK YOUR MEDIOCRITY.

THE SAFETY OF SOUND DOCTRINE

The world we are living in seems to be whirling out of control. Mainly over the fact that this world doesn't have a handle on the right doctrines about this life and the life to come. Many folks today step back when anyone seems to be very strong regarding doctrine.

Our world does not want anything that might cause them to be challenged, which would require a drastic change in lifestyles. I must stand strong in the fact that the message preached by most churches doesn't come close to the call made by Jesus and His apostles. The message from the start was one of challenge, change and total commitment to the Master and the message. Our soft living seems to be seeping into our churches and, in an effort to be popular and easy, doctrines that demand death to the flesh, constant crucifying and humbling, are just not what this world wants nor will stand still for. Our great Lord Jesus loved this world but He did not, nor will ever, come to terms with it in order to save it. He will require the new birth, holy living and doctrines that adorn holiness and nothing less will be accepted.

The truth shall make you free! That means the person and the precept, for the epistles were sent to saved folks, not the unsaved. We must be instructed in the right way to live and the right things to believe and the right way to get into His Kingdom. The new birth gets us in, doctrine helps us grow and stay saved.

Paul told Timothy to take heed to the doctrine for He would save himself and those that heard him. I must adhere to the APOSTLES DOCTRINE to PLEASE GOD AND ACCOMPLISH MY MISSION.

TASTING OF THE WORLD TO COME

The writer of Hebrews uses the above statement with regard to the experience of the NEW BIRTH.

The present world that we are passing through is actually the secondary world; the spirit world has always been the primary. The things which are seen were made from and by another world, with God being the power and source of both worlds. Two worlds now exist side by side, interacting and also affecting each other. The wonderful gift of the Holy Ghost is from another world, causing all who receive this experience to be partakers of something from beyond the present world. I am so glad that the Lord of Glory has allowed us to taste in this present day, some of the other world, which will never fade nor pass. The more we allow the Holy Ghost to work in our lives, the greater will be our desire to be conformed to that world while we still operate in this world. Jesus once told the people of His day that He was from above and not of this world. That is one reason we need to pay close attention to all He has told us and commanded. He knows more about time, matter, space, eternity, devils, judgment, heaven and hell. No wonder He told us to be born again, to taste the powers of the world to come and to be full of the spirit. He knew we would need the power to live in this world and to get to the next one.

May God help each one of us to become hungry and thirsty for all the world to come has to offer us while we move through this present world.

THE WORD WAS MADE FLESH: GOD EXPRESSED

The God of Glory has gone on record as being one who delights to express Himself through various methods and demonstrations. Being so full of power and wisdom, He seems to take great pains to show the world and creatures of other places His greatness expressed.

The Word tells us the heavens declare the glory of God and earth shows His handiwork. God has always left some type of witness regarding Himself but none as glorious as the word made flesh. When God put on the robe of flesh and walked among his creation, devils and nature recognized who was among them but mankind for the most part remained blind and deaf. The wonderful events that transpired at the cross and grave made it possible for the word to become flesh within all humanity. For the work of reconciliation required blood to allow the work of spiritual rebirth to occur. Calvary must precede Pentecost because God works legally. The separation sin caused had to be dealt with, and was, by the shed blood of Jesus, to allow God to communicate life to the believer. His spirit is life, called the Holy Ghost, and is actually the nature of God coming to live within our bodies.

The real purpose of preaching and the gospel is to get the word to become flesh, to allow the power of the word to become a part of our everyday living so we will be ambassadors for Christ. The word must impact us, call us to higher turf, send us to our knees to repent and receive mercy. God only confronts us to get us to see as He does, then be convicted to the place we will confess and forsake the things that offend God. He wants us to be like Him, to partake of His ways and wants for our good is behind all He talks to us about. May the Word become flesh.

THE LADDER LINKED TWO WORLD'S TOGETHER

Most children have heard often the story of the ladder of Jacob and what happened that night as he ran away from a bad situation. I know that the ladder was a link between two realms that encouraged that runaway lad that night. He must have been so lonely and lost; guilt and fear had traveled all that day with him. God showed such mercy and care to have let Jacob dream that night and see a ladder between two places, with angels going up and down and the Lord Himself standing at the top. We are made to realize that there is another world besides ours and we are quite noticed by it. Really, we are very cared about and that is reason for joy. Jesus would later tell the followers that they would see those same angels coming and going on him just like that ladder. Jesus was saying that he was the link with the other world, that the supernatural was very active on him and in him and through him. He was the doorway to and from that other world and what He was doing was of great importance.

Today, the church has also become the link and ladder for this world into the other world. The same spirit that was in and on Jesus has been given to the believer. We now are the only real and legal link to the spirit world. God has chosen to use the church as His very special vehicle of expression, much like the body of Jesus was long ago. What a great honor and responsibility has been given to us. We must stay in union with the heavens so the will of heaven will be revealed to the world. May God help us to be the link that leads others to the Lord of the ladder and magnify His great name.

I'M GETTIN' READY TO LEAVE THIS WORLD

The typewriter I am using sent me a signal when I had finished with the word gettin', informing me that I had misspelled the word. How like many we meet, so quick to inform us of mistakes made, to tell us we used the wrong word or show us they were listening for errors, never happy about the truth. The title of this article comes from one of the old songs in the Pentecostal Praise List. We must make sure we are indeed 'GETTIN' READY TO LEAVE THIS WORLD.'

One purpose of revival is to arouse and alert the church to our need to get closer to the Lord, become aware of the late hour we are living in and give us a fresh hunger for the saving of souls around us.

The Bible shows clearly that there is another world to come. It is in place now and by the grace of God we can taste of it through the new birth. Jesus often told the folks of His day, "Be watchful, be ready and keep yourself on the right path for in an hour you think not, He had promised to come again." We must live our lives as looking for His appearing and yet try to provide for our families as if He may not come for a long time. Living ready for the rapture must become primary with us, for to miss the catching away of the church would be the worst disaster any believer could experience.

May God help each one to use these days to examine our hearts, agendas, desires, dreams and spiritual state so that day will not catch us unawares. God will take no pleasure in our missing the very thing we have lived for and longed for. Allow the presence of God to impact you. Let His word examine you, your praying change you and you will be getting ready to leave this world. Glory!

OUR BEST DECISION – I AM NOT GOD

I know that most people would never speak outright and say they thought they were actually God, but when we seek to GOVERN our LIVES, SEEK ONLY OUR WILLS and ACT AS IF WE DETERMINED ALL, WE SURELY APPOINT OURSELVES AS LORD OF OUR LIVES.

To be dependent seems to go against the AMERICAN IDEA and attacks our EGO which we don't enjoy. When we were living unto ourselves in SIN, we were really being a GOD unto ourselves, but as we REPENTED and CONFESSED OUR SINS, we made a great admission that we were DUST and not DEITY. Our grasping of our needs is so healthy to our spiritual well being that God usually sees to it in life that we are forced to stay in that position.

I reread the account of the making of BEN-HUR and Charlton Heston's concern over the chariot race. He told the boss, Cecil D. DeMille, I think I can drive convincingly but I don't think I can win. DeMILLE Replied, YOU MUST DRIVE, I'LL DO THE REST. As the DIRECTOR, he had the ability to make Heston win the race and so does the LORD. He directs our steps and we must trust Him with the results of our race.

God provides the initial INPUT, we then provide the OUTPUT and God provides the OUTCOME. He has the power and wisdom to help us win the race. We must trust Him to help us WIN THE RACE. For He that has begun a good work in us, will finish it.

WHO IS LIKE THEE OH LORD?

These words were spoken by Moses after the nation had crossed the Red Sea and their enemies (the Egyptians) had tried and had been drowned. Moses began to extol the Lord and His great power and mercy shown to them. Who could open a sea, hold tons of water upright and allow passage thru those water walls, then cause them to come down upon their former captors? The God of Moses is also our Lord and God. Today there is still NONE LIKE UNTO HIM. He loves us with a PERFECT LOVE and as surely as He brought all of us out of sin with His Mighty Hand, He will make sure that we enter the place He has ordained for us. No matter the stack of problems, negatives that assault us, the disappointments that seek to discourage us.

FAITHFUL IS HE WHO HAS PROMISED, WHO WILL ALSO DO IT. Praise God! It is always wise to honestly appraise any situation and see what resources might be available. We must surely look unto OUR GOD who is able to accomplish all we cannot. Our ADVERSARY may seem unbeatable but our ALLY is really unbeatable. NOTHING IS IMPOSSIBLE TO HIM. Goliath may seem so huge, unbeatable, scary but our God is much bigger, greater and wiser than any foe we must deal with. Just look over your shoulder and count all the times He has rescued you, made a way when there seemed to be none, helped you get through this or that. Your faith will begin to rise anew and your fears will diminish for sure.

I thank God for HIS WORD, SPIRIT, BLOOD, THRONE OF GRACE, ANGELS WHO HELP US and for HIS UNCHANGING BEING. You can count on HIM to be all He has ever been and to trust Him to stay with us all the way. Oh Lord, WHO IS LIKE UNTO THEE? NONE!

BE THOU FAITHFUL UNTO DEATH

The Lord has put a great deal of value in being FAITHFUL to His cause, His word and His people. Our world does not value the trait of FAITHFULNESS like it once did, as various news stories relate often to us. I know that the world is surely ANTICHRIST in its thinking but the BELIEVER must resist the peer pressure to conform and go along with this sad state of affairs. When the courts allow something and even make it an acceptable practice, we who are believers must adhere strictly to HIS WORD and walk worthy of HIS CALLING.

We are being challenged daily to be FAITHFUL to the teachings of the book, and to be practicing the grand truths regardless of the pressure exerted by the UNBELIEVER. God has not said we must be SUCCESSFUL, OUTSTANDING, FAMOUS or ACCEPTED. He has called each of us to be FAITHFUL. That puts His request within the reach of every person on the planet. Anyone can purpose in their hearts to walk in the PATHS of GOD, for God has promised to assist any and all who seek to please Him.

God has promised a CROWN of LIFE to those who will stay true to Him and His purposes. Our day is so full of pressure and pleasures that one can find easy excuse for missing church, never getting involved or even in areas such as TITHING and GIVING. None can offer God the various excuses that they offer to the PREACHER, OTHERS or THEMSELVES. Folks know that JESUS WON'T BUY IT. May the Lord deliver each of us from DECEPTION. AMEN.

IT IS OVER ONLY WHEN WE QUIT

There are so many times we hear various statements regarding the finish of this or that. The real truth is that nothing is really over until we take the position that nothing else can be done or we accept defeat as final. To be defeated in any situation doesn't mean that it is over. It is ONLY OVER WHEN WE QUIT. I have had many things go wrong, lots of critics and probably many were correct to some degree. The devil often taunts me with the things my life is lacking, pointing out the flaws and failings in my plans and efforts. PRAISE GOD, by HIS GRACE I HAVE NOT QUIT!

Failure, setbacks and pain can truly serve to help us look again at areas of our lives and make tough decisions and changes that are needed. No one wants to change, but when we are honest about any area of life that needs help, we must force adjustment or sentence OURSELVES to more of the same. At times when the need for change looms ahead of me, I want to quit, but that is not what is needed. I must alter and believe that God has in His kindness caught my attention so GROWTH and MATURITY WILL OCCUR. Anyone can cry "WHAT IS THE USE?" But there is a reason for the challenge facing all of us. I thank God for every person, problem and pain that causes me to look deeper and clearer into my own life and use the gift of HUMAN CHOICE to try harder to become who and what I need to be.

I have often FAILED MISERABLY but I thank God for HIS GRACE and MERCY and also for many of you who have cared for me and prayed for me. THANK YOU SO MUCH. Keep loving me, praying for me and, by all means, DON'T QUIT. WORK THROUGH IT EVEN THOUGH YOU'RE CRYING.

MY WAYS ARE NOT YOUR WAYS

This title is one that seems to be repeated constantly in the WORD OF GOD and also IN OUR LIVES. God has always chosen those things, ways and people that none of us would have. I know that He seems to get great delight in using PEOPLE who seem to be so weak and rather insignificant to say the least. No one in business, government or sports would ever put their worst effort, personnel or programs into the fight first. But God seems to enjoy using those of us who are far from strong, not very wise and surely not qualified to accomplish HIS WORK, yet that is exactly HIS WAY.

He likes to take our weakness and magnify HIS POWER, our smallness, HIS GREATNESS, our ignorance with HIS WISDOM. God is determined that He will use all our failures, mistakes, and fears to show the world, the devil and us that HE IS ABLE TO DO ANYTHING HE WISHES WITH ANYTHING HE HAS CHOSEN. For with God, nothing is too hard.

The strange ways of God can at times cause the best of us some real problems, especially when we seem to think there was a much better, easier and less painful way of getting the job done. But God who sees the end from the beginning has a reason for all He does and WHY He does it that way. I may not grasp but I am required to trust Him though I can't seem to understand. I know from looking over my shoulder that many times what seemed to be crazy has now become so clear. I have to believe that He won't fail us now. I choose to stay with Him and His Ways even when I am confused. FOR GOD IS ALWAYS GOOD AND THAT IS ENOUGH.

GOD IS ABLE TO– THAT IS ENOUGH

To so many the obstacles of life seem to steal all hope and Joy from their very souls. These things should not be so with the BELIEVER. Our vision and understanding about God should cause all of us to lock our faith into HIS ABILITY rather than to shake in fear about our inability. I know that life is bigger than me and I shall be called upon to deal with things that are hard to handle, and tough to whip, but NOT TOO HARD FOR MY GOD! I must constantly lift my eyes UNTO HIM from whom all true riches and blessings flow. I know that I am weak, given to fears, limited in both resource and power, but the ONE that saved me, lives within me and has purposed for me to become victorious, IS MORE THAN ABLE.

Like the battery cables in the car, I must make connection with POWER so that I can function properly and accomplish the plan HE HAS SET FOR ME. I am not in this episode by myself, the Lord who called me out of darkness is also walking with me and has promised not to leave me nor to put anything on me that would totally destroy me or my faith. I know that at times the load has caused me to stumble, to feel tired and frustrated but this also has served to show me how much I need HIS POWER to make it. God who loved me enough to come to this planet and die in the body of JESUS CHRIST will not forsake me even though I fail often. He is too great, good and faithful to do anything else.

All through our lives we will face the fact of not having enough or not being enough, BUT OUR GOD IS MORE THAN ENOUGH.

GOD RESISTS THE PROUD

I read a wonderful sentence the other day that so impacted me that I want to share it now. "God only sends those away who are full of themselves, all others receive from him."

I know that God hates PRIDE but to be self satisfied must also move Him to anger seeing that all of us are so in need of HIS DAILY MERCIES. Our world system is constantly trying to get us to distrust God and become totally independent. No wonder there is such a clash between the TWO KINGDOMS. Pride can be so cleverly hidden under the robes of our just trying to get ahead or be less dependent or whatever, we must keep our guard up and our knees bent in prayer. So many folks who are very sincere are also very wrong in their approach to various situations.

As some of us approach mid–life we may have a tendency towards security and a way of life that can be just another form of PRIDE and SELF CARE. I know we all want to be taken care of and none of us really want to be in need yet it is in this very area that the LORD seems to clash with our concepts. He constantly kept ISRAEL just a day away from hunger and always kept them looking for the next load of MANNA. The PROPHET told the widow the BARREL would not go EMPTY but neither was it EVER FULL, always enough for the day. Maybe that is the reason behind, "GIVE US OUR DAILY BREAD."

I personally like it much better when I have some extra but that feeling has never one time produced a FRESH TRUST IN GOD, but a security from me. God is still drawn to need, empty and partial, but the FULL are still left to themselves.

THIS IS THE VICTORY

All of us surely enjoy victory over any type of defeat, the taste of victory is much sweeter. The Bible tells us that we are in a great battle, for our souls, the souls of others and for the HONOR of GOD. The Word tells us the avenue to our victory that overcomes the world is OUR FAITH. We are called upon often to believe when all the signs point the other way and the evidence seems to shout at us, YOU MUST BE CRAZY!

We are not called upon to ignore the facts, findings and etc., but rather to view them through the eye of faith. I can handle anything if I can lift my eyes off the mess and look at the MASTER. It is when I fail to do this, my feelings challenge me, my reason stomps on me, my fears arise and laugh at me and the things I read in the Word seem so UNREAL. I know that our FAITH must be TESTED and the TRIAL of OUR FAITH is usually not a quick, painless, joyful episode. When we are in the battle the pain, the strain, the foes are very real and very determined to defeat us. But GREATER is HE that is in ME than HE that is FIGHTING AGAINST ME.

Surely as there could be no crown for JESUS without a cross, no remission unless he had shed blood, no Holy Ghost without a resurrection, we cannot taste any type of true victory without a real fight. I am not able in myself, but thanks be to GOD I am not in this by myself. I may feel alone, but I am not, for He is with me through it all. I must trust when I can't trace, believe tho' I can't feel and stay when I want to leave.

FOR ALL THINGS ARE POSSIBLE THROUGH FAITH.

HOW DO YOU SPELL RELIEF?

How wonderful it is at different times in life to experience some type of relief from pain, pressure or whatever. I know that just a simple headache can just about drive one crazy and to have some relief seems just grand. I know that pain in the body, back, legs or joints can be horrible and to get some relief is so nice. There is a greater area we need to experience RELIEF in and that is in the SPIRITUAL ARENA. There is such a great sense of relief we can have when we UNDERSTAND GOD RULES IN ALL THINGS.

Joseph knew the blessing of RELIEF when he saw that the HAND of GOD was in the awful situation he had been through. He didn't allow himself to become bitter because UNDERSTANDING gave him RELIEF. I think lots of times I have not had the relief I could have had simply because I have not been able to grasp the RELIEF VALVE of UNDERSTANDING. Paul said the bad treatment that had occurred to him was for the furtherance of the work of God and thus the pain and pressure didn't destroy nor distract him, it helped to DEVELOP him. I must believe that MY TIMES ARE IN HIS HANDS, SEASONS ARE LIMITED AND RULED BY HIM, and that nothing is accidental. They are all APPOINTED for me. Jesus despised the cross, but he had Joy because he knew he would rise again, and the pain was part of the process required.

May God help all of us to have some type of RELIEF THROUGH UNDERSTANDING THINGS.

WE OWE SUCH A GREAT DEBT TO OUR DEAD

This weekend is celebrated nation wide as a remembrance for all the fallen dead of past wars. Wars that took from all people their loved ones, yet what could have been taken if they had not loved freedom as much as they did. No one wants folks to die in battle yet there roams on this planet many wicked and sick thinking folks who seem to want the enslaving of any and all who do not feel as they do. I am so THANKFUL for all those precious folks who lost their lives for many who lived elsewhere. What a great debt of gratitude we owe to so many that have gone on before us. THANK GOD FOR THEM.

Two thousand years ago another sacrifice was made for the souls of mankind. A death occurred that affected the entire universe. Jesus of Nazareth took on the devil on his own turf, totally whipped him, then allowed himself to be crucified and buried only to rise the third day. His dying was for OUR RECONCILING TO GOD, for the FORGIVING OF ALL OUR SINS. I was an outlaw before the THRONE of GOD with no right of appeal, so HE DIED IN MY PLACE so I could receive MERCY and PARDON. His dying was not in vain, for I have responded in repentance and water baptism in JESUS NAME and have received the Gift of the Holy Ghost. I am glad beyond words for this wonderful gift of FORGIVENESS and INFILLING that has come to me FROM THE BATTLEFIELD OF GLORY. I don't ever want to forget where I have come from, nor what HE did for me.

Let us take time to remember the FALLEN DEAD and most of all, the ONE WHO WAS DEAD BUT IS ALIVE.

MY YOKE IS EASY AND VERY NEEDFUL

So many times we hear this verse used and yet we seem to overlook that the ease of the yoke does not allow us to disregard the need of that yoke. Any life that will end up counting must be yoked to various things, one of which is DENIAL OF SELF. I know the generation of today hates to hear any type of DENIAL for we are so rights and liberty unbalanced, we just simply balk and squawk at DENIAL.

If a horse is going to win a race or plow a field, it must be HARNESSED to accomplish some purpose, it can't just do as it pleases. No life can ever grow GREAT without first being dedicated, focused and disciplined. Apostle Paul told us many times that the YOKE PRINCIPLE has to be in effect if we expect to win the race we are called to run.

Jesus told us to take up OUR CROSS, after we had DENIED OURSELVES. Any athlete, artist, inventor, builder can take the witness stand and verify the truth that without some type of YOKE in place, the end result will not be as one hoped for. I am sure that the YOKE being offered to all believers is the best thing that Jesus has to offer us as we seek to do HIS WORK WITH Him and for HIM. He spent his whole life in the YOKE of HEAVEN and look what He has accomplished for the human race. Oh how much He denied Himself in order to grant GRACE, MERCY and ETERNAL LIFE to humanity.

Considering the WONDERFUL PERSON who calls us into this YOKE WITH HIM. We should respond with surrender and expectation that HE has some grand plan for us with Him.

THE BLESSINGS OF REAL TROUBLE

I want you to grasp the difference between real trouble and various irritations in life. Your toe may be hurting you but if you break it or lose use of it, your outlook will change drastically. There are surely different levels of trouble but trouble itself can be a great blessing. You may ask "Why?" Well, I can explain. Trouble has the ability to reveal our limitations and inadequacy about the situation and yet reveal HOW GREAT GOD IS.

Obstacles have a way of showing to us and yet helping our vision to be lifted off ourselves and onto the Lord. He has told us numerous times in the Bible to look unto Him in the time of trouble and if we could cry unto Him, He would step in and help us. God uses the problem as a platform to display His power and care for us, although we often think He hasn't gotten involved fast enough. God loves us unconditionally and does not want us to get frantic, bitter or worse, to start blaming God for things that go haywire. I have been through some things and have failed to handle it properly but God has been so faithful and kind. He lets me try again–ha–ha!

The old song used to say, "Thru it all I have learned to trust in Jesus." The real message is on the words, I have learned...I know the learning time can be painful but when we look back, we will be so much better for the trouble, it will be called a blessing.

May God help each of us as we go through and learn more of Him and about ourselves.

FOR SUCH A TIME AS THIS

These are the words given to Esther from her uncle with regard to the present crisis that had unfolded for the Jewish people who were a part of the Persian empire at that time. Haman, a hater of the Jews, had just received permission to destroy them and her uncle brought her before the king to seek for mercy, being told that she has been put into a key position by God for such a time as this. Many times we are in places that seem so insignificant but God, who knows all things, puts us just where we can be of the most good in some crisis. Esther had not told anyone she was Jewish but now it was time for her to reveal that and by being the Queen, she would have access to the King to accomplish some great work for God.

Is it possible that you and I have been ordained by God for this very hour? He has planned all along to have us matched with this generation. God can never be caught unprepared by any situation so whatever we find ourselves in, it was the Lord who has done so for His Glory and Work. People we have come to know, positions we have been put into, skills we have acquired, are all things that God can use for His Grand Purpose. We must be aware of our responsibility to step forward and get involved. It is really a great honor for us to be put into any place or position so we can be a witness for His Name. Joseph was put into a mess so God would have someone on site who could then impact an entire kingdom and save nations. Moses was raised in Egypt to learn its ways, then driven from it to learn the ways of God. Daniel was taken hostage and carried away but God used him to affect that world. Can we see through faith, how God works things into our lives so we can be a part of His plan?

SUBMISSION BRINGS VICTORY

The world we live in does not take too kindly to anything that smacks of restraint, rules or submitting to any type of authority. To me this attitude is a revelation of how far mankind has fallen from Adam's original place before he also decided to abandon the posture of submission to ALMIGHTY GOD. As long as Adam stayed submitted, he had all the authority needed to do the will of God. Once he left that place, he experienced defeat in numerous areas. Submission is not a terrible thing as taught today, it is not defeatism nor dishonorable, but rather wisdom at work.

When we honor God in bending to His wishes we then defeat our adversary who bas been whipped by his own inability in this area We are totally inferior to God yet He wants to enlist us in His work. Being all-wise, all-powerful, all-knowing, ever-present and eternal, He doesn't need anything we could do for Him. Yet He seems to take pleasure In working with us and in us. In submitting we actually partake of His power and thus become much more than we could ever be in our own ability. We are told to SUBMIT TO GOD, RESIST THE DEVIL AND HE WILL FLEE FROM US. Too many believers seek to quote verses, pray prayers of command or even attack the foe without first submitting to God. We are no match for Satan, even with various gifts we may possess, unless we are in submission to God, for then we have His protection. We are aware we didn't do it and pride cannot be used to defeat us. His power is made perfect in our weakness, and when we are weak, then are we really strong, for His strength comes into our situations.

May Jesus help us to desire to be submitted to God, His leaders and to each other, then victory!

JESUS WENT ABOUT DOING GOOD & HEALING ALL

Jesus spent his time in the affairs of others doing good to them, which was not always applauded or appreciated. The Bible tells us that God is so totally good and He lets it rain on the just and the unjust, the sun shines for the corrupt and the pure in heart. Jesus was God in a body doing what comes natural to God, being good and doing good no matter who received that kindness. We are told to be followers and imitators of our Lord Jesus, so our calling is very simple: doing good to all men, especially to those of the household of faith. There are so many folks who are in desperate need of some type of goodness and that gesture is within the reach of every one of us. It requires no special training, no spiritual gifting nor any special level of education. God has told us what pleases Him and manifests His nature to this world: doing good to all men everywhere.

While this sounds so simple it is much more trying and difficult than it seems. We all wish good treatment and usually expect it when we have done good to folks, but this does not always occur. Often we get taken advantage of or misread or even mistreated even when we tried to be kind; this is part of bearing the yoke and reproach of the believer. Jesus did help and heal all who were being oppressed by the devil but that didn't carry much weight with the crowds when His doctrine rubbed them the wrong way. Yet even dying on the cross, He prayed for those who were mistreating Him because He knew they didn't understand what they were doing. On the cross, He was doing good for all of us, dying in our place so we could be saved. How good our God is always.

May God grant us the grace to do good to any and all, in the Spirit of Jesus Christ. Be a Do–Gooder!

I MUST BE ABOUT MY FATHERS BUSINESS

These words fell from the lips of our Lord when He had been found by his parents after being gone for 3 or 4 days. They did not appreciate nor really grasp all that he meant with those words, for they revealed his inner drive and desires. Jesus felt that the work of God was the utmost and it should have his attention first and foremost. HE MUST DO IT.

Have you ever felt that way about the things of God? I just have to do something. I must take time to pray today, I must read the word more than I have been, I must tell someone about what God has done for me and to me. I must be about HIS BUSINESS with a greater drive and desire than I put into my own affairs. For His work is everlasting, mine is limited to time. How many times have we all said I MUST do this or that, I MUST get the house cleaned, I MUST fix that broken object, I MUST get this finished, etc. and etc. We all can identify with those things we MUST do in life but what about the GREATEST MUST, the things of the kingdom?

After burying various relatives and friends over the years I have noticed many things. I have seen folks change priorities when a sickness or tragedy comes, when they are injured and can't perform as before. THOSE THINGS THAT WERE A MUST now seem to become secondary. I know we all battle with getting things done, with determining what gets our attention and what gets put on the back burner.

I pray that we can get that feeling and action into our lives like Jesus. I MUST DO HIS WORK FIRST.

THE DEVIL'S MOST SUCCESSFUL MINISTERS

All of us are really interested in some type of success and so is the devil, yet he seems to be helped by folks that should be his greatest problem rather than ASSET. His most helpful workers, ministers and ambassadors are ANY and ALL WHO ARE INCONSISTENT ABOUT THEIR WALK WITH THE LORD. Jesus told us that a tree is known by its fruit and so must each person who professes to be saved from sin. We who have been blessed to be forgiven and filled with the HOLY GHOST must maintain a high standard of actions and attitudes for our great KING. We are such debtors to grace and mercy and we may be the only BIBLE any unbeliever may gaze upon. May our WALK MATCH OUR TALK.

What SORT of SERMON have we preached this week at the office, school or places we have eaten at? A sermon doesn't need a pulpit to be powerful or harmful. Just allow yourself to be inconsistent and we end up doing so much damage. We offer our enemy a platform to show the lost that JESUS doesn't really count in the lives of church folks. We are all called to be steadfast, unmovable and abounding in the work of the LORD, not in helping our enemy to TEAR DOWN THE LORD. David's sin was terrible regarding Bathsheba, but the prophet told him the real tragedy was that he had now allowed through his actions A GREAT REPROACH TO BE CAST UPON GOD. None of us, I am sure, would do anything that would hurt the cause of heaven but through our inconsistencies we do help the one who hates both Jesus and His church.

May God help all of us to be very careful with our walk, talk and actions so we do not become an asset to our enemy and a shame to our Lord.

BE YE THANKFUL IN ALL THINGS

Paul tells us that we should give thanks in everything, for this is the will of God in Christ Jesus concerning you. Sometimes this is easier spoken than lived. Amen! No one enjoys various problems and situations that try you to the breaking point but I know that in spite of aggravations and setbacks, God Is Good every day, All The Time. I have lived long enough in this great way of holiness and truth to shout aloud that nothing shall separate me from the love of God. Nothing! When we are called upon to taste bitter things, unfair things, undeserved things, we should all realize that the LORD has allowed each of us to show forth His praise in that problem, mess, or bad treatment and glorify Him with our actions and attitudes.

In my own life I have been made to see that many areas still need much more work, and being loved by Jesus as much as I am, He is making sure I get all the attention needed to help crucify those areas. Ha! Ha!

God is so faithful to what He has begun in each of our lives, He knows what is required to form us and shape us into the vessels that will bring Him honor and magnify His grace in our lives. I have not been very happy of late, bleeding quite a bit over various things, but I reflect on how much I have to be thankful for and how blessed I really am. In fact, I think all the grief that has been assigned to me of late is a vote from Him that I am being worked on and that I am cared for by Him. Our generation bears the curse of being unthankful which breeds all sorts of disasters and various conduct perversions as shown in Romans 1. May God help all of us to be Thankful for Life, Health, Provision, Family and Salvation.

I WILL LIFT UP MINE EYES UNTO THE HILLS

The above words have been a constant challenge to all of us during times of problems, pains and perplexity. Found in these words is the formula for victory in any situation. For to look unto the hills one must take their eyes off the situation they have been looking at. The obvious always challenges us and reason jumps on board to really try to sink our ship of faith. Remember; untested faith should not be trusted, our faith must stand the test. God never allows anything into our lives with the purpose of destroying us but rather for developing us by allowing a discovery to occur.

Often in trouble we will find out something about ourselves that we had been unaware of prior to the problem. Even in our seeming disasters, our God and King orders the episodes so we may mature and magnify His grace. The next part of the quote says from whence cometh my help. Cometh means continual coming, constant arrival of fresh help and grace. The rest of the verse says, our help comes from the Lord that made Heaven and earth. It becomes totally impossible for any of us to stay in despair when we understand that our helper is omnipotent, all powerful, almighty and that he loves us always.

Remember the next time you get confronted with a crisis, your helper is awesome and does not desire your failure or fears. I must fight daily to redirect my focus from off the obvious to the invisible but that is exactly where our help will come from.

THE REAL TRUTH ABOUT WINNING AND LOSING

All of us want to be winners at the game of life, but sometimes we make the mistake in thinking that life is a game and nothing could be further from the truth. This thing called life is anything but a game, for after death we continue to exist in spirit form. The Bible says, after death, then the judgment. Another writer says it is a fearful thing to fall into the hands of the living God. Another writer tells us that some men's sins go before them and others have their sins following them.

I have seen the bumper sticker that says, "He that dies with the most toys wins." What a terrible lie hell has hatched with those words. The Lord Jesus tells we that life consists not in the abundance of the things we possess, regarding the material world. The real truth is that to lose our soul and win the world means we are big losers. The Lord said that the world itself compared to the worth of our souls would not be a fair exchange. Oh that God would help each of us to get the proper scales with which to measure life with. Better to be a pauper and rich in spirit and truth than to own most of the world and be bankrupt in your spiritual bank account. To win eternal life makes any and all the real winners and we must fight against the perverted concepts the world around us constantly spews out through the printed page, radio or television.

To be born again, to be in the kingdom of God, to put the Lord Jesus first and serve His pleasures will make us wise though the world looks with disdain upon our so called stupidity. To be like Jesus Christ Is the finest wisdom and glory to be had and when this world has fallen into eternal punishing, the redeemed will be the new owners of it all: The real winners.

SUPER DIVINE SUPERNATURAL IS NEEDED

How many times do we either say or hear the word SUPER, meaning something is cool, great or has worked out for the best in some situation. We say the look of a car, clothes, houses, numerous other things is SUPER and church services, SUPER, but real Christianity must be SUPERNATURAL. Most folks who go to some type of church service like them to be nice, not too noisy, very entertaining and somewhat brief, but without the SUPERNATURAL POWER OF GOD. The services are simply a sham substitute for the real purpose of services. When believers come together it may include music, songs, preaching and praying but the power from above must be allowed to operate and impact. Simply put, we must stretch ourselves beyond what our flesh, our minds and thoughts enjoy and experience the glory world now. Most so called believers accept the next world to come as being greater and more glorious than ours today but they very seldom seek to step into that realm and taste of its miraculous menu.

Pentecost was and still is a glorious supernatural happening and we must really contend for the power of God in our lives and church services, for nothing else is able to bring change to our being. Jesus required the early followers not to go out and represent Him until they had been filled with the Holy Ghost. Dare we accept a position any less than the original?

I am seeking God for a visitation of Himself that will so change us and empower us that we will become His story rather than just telling His story. REACH WITH ME–PLEASE.

THE IDEAL—
A GOD GOVERNED LIFE

God, who is altogether good at all times, who never once has, nor will ever fall below HIS BEST, does not seek to govern our lives to hamper, reduce or steal joy from any of us. God is the author of joy, gladness and holiness. He does not seek to rule us so we are His slaves and puppets but rather that we become lovers of HIM and His Ways. He who knows all things, all things I say, that in itself throws us such a curve, for nothing nor any type of person on this planet knows everything so we have no level of comparison which always creates discomfort to us. God knows what is best, knows what lies ahead, the various tricks of the enemy so He desires to create within us a yearning to comply with HIS PLANS for He knows they alone contain fullness of joy to all who will walk therein.

God loves me too much to let me walk in my ways, for the word says, "It is not in man to direct his step" and I have lived long enough to say AMEN to that truth. I want to bring every facet of my life in line with His WORD so that I will show Him that I do HONOR and LOVE HIM. Jesus told us in John14: IF YOU LOVE ME, KEEP MY COMMANDMENTS. The proof of really loving God is to do to the best of our ability what God has told us, either through His word or through His appointed delegated leaders.

Our day is filled with resentment towards any type of rulership, authority or restraint but God has put into His body Pastors to feed His sheep, to challenge the flock, to rebuke error, exhort to good works and godliness. May God help each of us to seek to be governed which requires us to support His church, to attend to teaching, to submit to Leadership.

THE BUILDING IS DONE, THE WORK HAS BEGUN

Many thanks to all the grand folks from our church family who worked so hard to make the dedication services a grand time for all. My heart is full of thanks to you; no pastor could be more awed and moved by such a display of real service and dedication. So many of the visiting ministers commented on the wonderful building, but more so on the fantastic people who served them in the Family Life Center and how beautiful the Center was done—wow, wow, and wow! I cannot express how I really feel, but I have never been so thankful for all of you. You are the best!

I know the best and biggest work now looms ahead of each of us seeking the lost and instructing many in the ways of God. I will do my best to be a clear voice for growth and revival and cast the vision for us the best I can. Please hold me up in your prayers. Please ask the Lord to touch your lives with a burden and boldness, for we are short on time and must be about His work. I know the God of Glory didn't help us to erect this building just to have a new place but rather through the process of doing it, we could become family and focused for the great work we have been called to do. Please pray for a fresh zeal to fulfill our purpose for being here; we must see souls brought out of darkness and impacted for His name sake. We are really His workmanship, created unto good works, and for the praise of His Glory. What a great honor we have to serve Him and His cause. To be fellow workers with God is not something to be taken lightly. Let your faith soar; God is among us...

THE PAST CAN BE VERY POWERFUL

We are often told not to look back but to look forward. However, this cannot apply to all things; for our YESTERDAYS are full of powerful pictures and emotions that can help or hinder the efforts of today. Memory has a wonder attached to it sometimes it can make us very afraid with guilt, very sad with sorrow, or happy and glad with joy and warmth. We must be selective with our past, not avoiding something because it hurt or because we tripped over some obstacle. That can become a place of reflection unto despair. We are told by GOD to REMEMBER where we came from, how terrible it used to be for us, how low we had gotten, and how GOOD GOD has been to us. The PAST can INSPIRE or DEFLATE, so we must choose wisely or we can HURT OURSELVES.

Today I have been in a battle in my mind regarding the WORK OF GOD, MY OWN MINISTRY, PERSONAL PROBLEMS, FRUSTRATED EFFORTS and a LACK OF SENSING DIRECTION for this assembly and myself. I have told all of you this to reveal a wonderful lesson I tasted today, that of ceasing the chase for answers and thanking God for all His past works, answers, kindness, faithfulness and blessings. I had enough of unanswered issues today, and so I stopped asking for direction and began to force praise & thanks for the past to leave my lips. This changed the whole outlook of my prayer time. I felt the only way to get the upper hand over my enemy and my flesh was to relive, recall, and review, the times in my past that have been rich with GOD. It was a grand time for me, and my enemy lost some ground in my THOUGHT LIFE as well. If any of you are beating yourselves against a wall or feeling frustrated with no progress, stop the parade and bring up some past episodes when God answered. It will fuel you for the fight!

THE COST OF CHRIST LIKENESS IS VERY HIGH

When we first became believers in Jesus, we were in search of freedom from habits, lifestyles and sins that had become forms of slavery. To meet Jesus and have our past forgiven, or the present changed into liberty was fabulous to say the least. I am concerned today with the lack of our understanding regarding the CALL OF GOD TO CONFORMITY TO CHRIST. I feel we must study once again exactly what we have gotten ourselves into when we were born into the KINGDOM. Much more than being set free from sins, we have now become HIS LIVING STORIES AND BILLBOARDS. We have been called to HIS CROSS to experience a death unto life, but we must really die to ourselves if we are to experience the FORCE OF REAL RESURRECTION. The SECURITY we all seek can only be found when we give ourselves away for HIS GLORY. There must be an end to SELF–LIVING. For that to happen, we must now EMBRACE THE CROSS OF PERSONAL DENIAL AND EXAMPLE HIS LIFESTYLE.

For the average believer, what I am now speaking about is totally foreign and not very acceptable; but it is really the way of the KINGDOM LIFE. He must INCREASE AND I MUST DECREASE. Anything less than this must be seen as FALSE CHRISTIANITY. We are called not only to believe and submit to THE APOSTLES DOCTRINE but also to LIVING IN THE WAY THEY LIVED, DYING DAILY. The experience of the CROSS AND THE RESURRECTION must be seen and played out in the lives of believers. The world we live in must be confronted with SEEING GOD'S LOVE in the SELFLESS GIVING UP OF SELF. It is time for the CHURCH TO EXAMPLE CRUCIFIED LIVES to a world that lives only for itself. We MUST DIE TO SELF THAT JESUS CAN LIVE THOUGH US.

THERE IS A WAY THAT SEEMS RIGHT

The writer of Proverbs tells us that something may SEEM RIGHT, but it will only end in DEATH. How many times in our own lives have we done something we felt was RIGHT, but found out later it was totally WRONG? I know that life is a constant effort in learning RIGHT AND WRONG, but when it comes to SPIRITUAL WAYS, THE ABILITY TO TRY OVER DOESN'T PRESENT ITSELF if we walk in the wrong path. It could cost us our soul's welfare, and that is nothing to smile about. I know the age we live in smirks at anything that states ANYTHING IS ABSOLUTE, but the GOD OF GLORY doesn't play games when it comes to the RIGHT PATH, RIGHT WAY TO LIVE AND RIGHT WAY TO PLEASE HIM. Please notice; the writer said, "THERE IS A WAY THAT SEEMETH RIGHT." It just felt, looked and sounded right, but it led into the way of death. The BAIT is designed to HIDE THE HOOK; the DEVIL seeks to DECEIVE by making the TRUE WAY seem to be too hard, narrow or even too old fashioned for the modern man of today.

Please be advised, God wishes none to be lost or led astray but has made a way for any and all to walk in the right path. However, one must study, submit to some type of leadership and pray for direction lest we end up LOST FOREVER. We must not trust our feelings; they will fluctuate and fool us. Well meaning friends will advise us, but the TRUTH OF GOD is not up for ANYONE'S OPINION. Our upbringing can impact our viewpoint to the place we will become offended if it is challenged, but THE TRUTH IS STILL THE TRUTH REGARDLESS...

Jesus told us to follow HIM. He is the WAY, TRUTH, LIFE and He will give us the ability to KNOW HIS VOICE—just ask HIM.

IN EVERYTHING GIVE THANKS— THIS IS HIS WILL

When, the Apostle Paul wrote the Roman letter, he did an AUTOPSY of previous generations. Their cause of disaster was very easy to discover: NEITHER WERE THEY THANKFUL. . . Being THANKFUL contains within itself the ability to be DEPENDENT, HUMBLE and SEEKING. The person who can be THANKFUL though they might be suffering, being mistreated or just going thru situations, can defeat the devil much more easily because THANKFULNESS delivers from various attitudes that harm us. Not one person reading this neither likes to be taken for granted, nor used by someone. In the same manner, God doesn't appreciate any who are not THANKFUL. We live on HIS PLANET, BREATHE HIS AIR, USE HIS RESOURCES, ENJOY HIS BENEFITS; and then for us not to offer thanks, must surely be an INSULT of the worst kind. Being thankful has a way of reducing nasty things to their proper size and exalting God to His rightful place, KING OF KINGS, LORD OF LORDS.

Jonah shows us that it is not easy at times to be THANKFUL for unpleasant duties, but we must realize that DUTY IS A TASK BEFORE IT CAN BE A FEELING. If the feeling is there, the job doesn't seem so bad; but if we do not feel anything, the task can be a CHORE we despise. When anyone must serve someone they love or feel deeply for, the task does not irk them like it might have. With all that God has done for each of us, being THANKFUL should be easy. Plus the fact we FEEL about God with such deep emotions, DOING SHOULD BE NO TASK. Jesus said, IF YOU LOVE ME, KEEP MY COMMANDMENTS. Our love for HIM should help us to do whatever HE WILLS without AGITATING US...IN EVERYTHING GIVE THANKS.

'TIS THE SEASON TO BE JOLLY

Well, that time of the year is once again upon us, the time for carols, parties, shopping for gifts, and sending cards to friends and loved ones, Wow, I AM GETTING TIRED ALREADY. Most of you know by now that the OLE WARDEN is not quite hep on all the HYPE of forced gift exchanging and the stuff usually associated with JINGLE BELLS. If we were really thrilled about who came to the earth 2000 years ago and what HE did for all of us, I am sure we would do our best to MAGNIFY HIM and INVEST into the WORK HE CAME TO ACCOMPLISH. I am not against giving or shopping; my concern each year is the LOSS OF JESUS during the SHAM OF SHOPPING AND SINGING. The wise men gave GIFTS TO HIM AND HIS FOLKS, should not we seek to at least emulate them in some degree??? What a wonderful time of the year to REVEAL the real meaning of the SEASON by celebrating the REASON FOR THE SEASON. I am sure some reading this will take offense, feeling I am out of touch with reality, but I must stand my ground for SATAN STALKS ALL THE SAINTS.

May God help all of us to show the SPIRIT OF CHRIST through the holidays and to seek to MANIFEST REAL JOY: the JOY OF BEING FILLED WITH THE HOLY GHOST, OF HAVING OUR SINS FORGIVEN, AND HAVING OUR NAMES WRITTEN IN THE BOOK OF LIFE. Amid all the craziness of this season let us reflect the grand GIFT OF GRACE that came wrapped in the FACE OF THAT BABY, our LORD AND KING WHO CAME TO SEE ABOUT US...

'TIS THE SEASON TO BE JOLLY EVERYDAY OF THE YEAR FOR GOD HAS COME TO LIVE WITHIN OUR SPIRITS! GLORY TO GOD FOREVER...

THE KING CAME: MANY ATTITUDES WERE SHOWN

Today marks the last SUNDAY OF '99, and we are part of making HISTORY. We should do all we can to apply the CHRISTMAS STORY to our lives. I know the gifts have been exchanged, get–togethers have occurred, and the JOY of the HOLIDAYS has been experienced. So we now live in the afterglow and must face the cold stark reality that the GREAT BUILDUP SEEMED GREATER THAN THE ACTUAL TIME; we must deal with the AFTER CHRISTMAS BLUES. May God help each of us to seek to be better folks with regard to areas in our lives that we know need REAL CHANGE. I am still moved by the fact that I am alive at this point in time, that I will face a new CENTURY packed with UNCERTAINTY, FEARS, WONDERS, and THE GREAT GOD OF GLORY WHO CHANGES NOT. He who kept us through all our varied situations will not fail us now; He has promised to be with us ALWAYS.

My wife and I want to THANK all who gave us an offering. Many we know gave sacrificially. We know you gave this in REAL LOVE AND CONCERN, and we are both moved by your gesture. We do APPRECIATE all the CHRISTMAS CARDS AND GIFTS that have come our way. Thank you once again for being so kind. May God Bless each of you…

The Bible says, "Better is the end of a thing than the beginning," and I am so glad we have come to the end of building this complex. You have been so wonderful in standing with me; your prayers and support have made a DIFFERENCE. I do not know what I would have done without all the help and encouragement. Now a new task lies before us, to touch the lost with this great message and see them saved. Let's do our part, God will do His.

REMEMBER...FORGET...GO FORWARD

WE have just left a century behind, a brand new one has just been handed to us, and it is full of grand opportunities to accomplish whatever we can for the LORD. As with ISRAEL OF OLD, we are called to REMEMBER the GOODNESS OF GOD shown to all of us last year. We need to RECALL how FAITHFUL GOD HAS BEEN even when we have failed to be faithful. We must look over our shoulder with gratitude for the GRACE that has been afforded us, to not only SAVE us, but for KEEPING us from all sorts of situations. REMEMBER...

We must also make a concerted effort to FORGET things that have tripped us, hurt us, attacked us, scared us, and annoyed us; for our enemy will try to use all the various things from our yesterdays to take us hostage and rob us of our JOY and FAITH. Forgetting some things that have happened is not always easy. The FEELINGS generated from those situations seem to live on and on, but we must take courage from THE WORD, "WHAT HAS BEEN FORGIVEN HAS BEEN FORGOTTEN." Once we repent of anything, God erases it from the record, but our MEMORY CIRCUITS like to REMIND us all over. FORGET THINGS THAT WILL NOT HELP YOU GO FORWARD IN GOD...

GO FORWARD, for progress requires that movement be involved to accomplish it. I must now greet this new day with FAITH AND HOPE and believe that GOD has really matched me with both the place and the time I find myself locked into. God, who makes no mistakes, has something grand ahead for us and this assembly, so I must not tarry too long. I MUST MOVE FORWARD.

WHO CAN TELL WHAT THE LORD MIGHT DO

Many times in the scriptures these words have been stated. Because we really don't know, we must attempt everything for the LORD. We are so prone to look at the OBVIOUS and seem to be totally blind to the INVISIBLE, that we miss the mighty things that GOD has wanted to do with us and for us. One writer spoke this way, "IT MAY BE THAT GOD WILL TURN AND LEAVE A BLESSING BEHIND." Those words should inspire us to believe that ALL THINGS ARE POSSIBLE WITH GOD.

When the FOUR LEPERS who had been sitting at the gate finally made a move, it was based on the assumption that God may give them favor with the enemies or just let them die. They didn't really know the OUTCOME but were willing to try something. I think that we all are very UNCERTAIN about the FUTURE, but we need not to be UNCERTAIN ABOUT GOD. The God we serve is still in CHARGE and has all the WISDOM AND POWER AND DESIRE needed to DO ABUNDANTLY ABOVE AND BEYOND ANYTHING THAT WE CAN EVEN THINK OR ASK... God is so full of SURPRISES that mankind has never been able to BOX HIM IN. He seems to DELIGHT in doing things beyond our human imagination, MAYBE BECAUSE HE ENJOYS BEING GOD ALMIGHTY.

I am persuaded by my past that God will do nothing outside HIS HOLY NATURE, nothing that would violate HIS GREATNESS. I know from the past that He is ABLE AND WILLING to HELP US, BLESS US AND USE US in spite of our fears or weak ways. God wants to use the PLATFORM OF OUR WEAKNESS to display HIS POWER and wills to show HIMSELF STRONG FOR THOSE WHO WILL ALLOW HIM TO. May God help each of us to EXPECT THE UNUSUAL and BELIEVE THE IMPOSSIBLE IS POSSIBLE, because we don't know how GOD WILL WORK, OR WHEN HE WILL MANIFEST HIMSELF.

SPEAK LORD FOR THY SERVANT HEARETH

The setting for this article comes from the calling of SAMUEL when he was just a lad. He had been working in the TEMPLE, but the Bible states that he did not yet know the Lord. It is so possible for many of us to be involved in the WORK OF THE LORD and never really get to KNOW THE LORD OF THE WORK. I realize that God must REVEAL HIMSELF to each person; but once He does so, it is very important that we give ourselves totally to Him. Samuel did not know what God was going to tell him, require of him, or what was about to happen; but he did at least tell God that he wanted to listen to the Lord. As we are called upon by God to do various things, surrender our control of areas of our lives, or whatever, may God grant us the willingness to want HIM to talk to us, with us, and through us.

All my CHRISTIAN LIFE I have desired for the VOICE OF GOD to impact me. I have often pleaded with Him that if He would just make HIS will plain to me, I would quickly respond and comply. The battle seems to be DISCERNING HIS VOICE, separating self from the issue, and being sure we are not being LED ASTRAY. I do not want to be hard of spiritual hearing, nor DECEIVED BY MYSELF, DEVILS, OR OTHERS. I must be able to grasp HIS WONDERFUL WORDS so I can do as He wishes. Too many folks have stopped hearing from the LORD, now they READ THE WORD, REMEMBER SOME EVENTS, and just live on. Jesus told us, "MY SHEEP HEAR MY VOICE." We must all strive to be SENSITIVE; for God wants to DIRECT US, INSTRUCT US, AND USE US for HIS PURPOSE. We cannot always count on what was fine last time or years ago; WE MUST HAVE A FRESH WORD FOR OUR LIVES.

POVERTY IS NOT THE LACK OF MONEY BUT THE LACK OF VISION

Vision, dreams, desires and hopes are the rich things in life, not having some money in your pocket or bank accounts. I have met some folks who had ample supply of finance who were below the POVERTY LEVEL regarding DREAMS AND VISIONS. Tomorrow flows from today, and today is made rich by our DREAMS AND VISION about the future. We were surely meant to live in our NOW, but only as we reflect on our PAST and see ahead into our FUTURE. I once read a statement that said, "THE POOREST PERSON IS NOT THE ONE WITHOUT ONE CENT BUT RATHER THAT ONE WHO EXISTS WITHOUT A DREAM OR VISION." To live only for today will surely leave us totally empty within our souls; for SPIRITUAL THINGS are the RICH THINGS IN LIFE. If we can see ahead to some goal or dream, then what we are forced to face now will not be able to destroy us, defeat us, or even drown us with despair.

Jesus faced the horror of the CROSS with the JOY of knowing SOMETHING WAS BEYOND THAT CROSS, THE RESURRECTION AND THE CHURCH. If we are locked into today only, we can feel like PRISONERS WITHOUT HOPE. So we must allow ourselves to LOOK BEYOND THE NOW. DREAMS can be a great avenue for fresh faith, hope and courage if we will do what we can to allow them to become expressed reality. Dreams will come to pass if you refuse to allow them to be stolen, or made fun of to the point we let them slip away.

It takes effort to make the vision a living thing. Sometimes you will be the only one who believes in it, but so what...DREAM BIG, FOR YOUR GOD IS MEASURELESS...

FIGHT THE GOOD FIGHT OF FAITH

Most of us know that we are engaged in a massive battle for our souls, but I wonder if we might be missing the REAL BATTLEFRONT. I know the devil stalks us, studies us, seeks to deceive us and finally destroy us, but I really think he is not the biggest battle I must face. Jesus told us that the devil had no place within Him that could be used to defeat Him. So it must be true that the battle rages WITHIN US FIRST AND FOREMOST. It is the SIN WITHIN, THE WEAKNESS WITHIN, THE DESIRES DEEP WITHIN, THE ATTITUDES WITHIN, THE FEARS WITHIN, THE WORRIES WITHIN, THE DRIVES DEEP WITHIN that seem to be the WAR ZONE for us. TRUE HOLINESS in its fullness is actually a life that is FULL OF LIGHT, HAVING N0 PART DARK. Jesus was such a person, having no area of His inward being blotched, smeared, or stained with any type of vileness. We are often told in the WORD to keep our HEARTS CLEAN, for out of them flow the ISSUES OF LIFE. The battle for us is forever THE FOE DEEP WITHIN our own hearts and emotions. I know for certain that to CONQUER MYSELF is greater than WHIPPING THE WORLD; for I am more valuable than the entire world. We are the reason for the CROSS.

Jesus died for us—not houses, lands, gold, silver, and jewels—but for our PRICELESS SOULS. All of us can at times defeat the biggest problems outside of us much easier than the little thing within us, and that is why the BATTLE WITHIN can become so frustrating. I can overcome things at times that might defeat men greater than myself, and yet some aspect of myself below the surface can knock me silly. Yet we must not grow weary with the warfare; for the outcome will be worth every denial we have been required to make. THE WORLD OF SELF IS STILL THE TOUGHEST PLACE TO CONQUER, but God is with us. So keep fighting everything opposite GODLINESS. It will be worth it…

FAITH WITHOUT WORKS IS DEAD BEING ALONE

Most of us understand that no one can be saved by WORKS. Yet once saved, WORKS are a mandate. We are thankful for the GRACE that affords the opportunity to be GRAFTED INTO the KINGDOM OF GOD, but once spared, we are RESPONSIBLE to our benefactor to do all we can for HIM AND HIS KINGDOM. We are facing the COMING OF THE LORD and we will give an account of the deeds done in the body and just how we used, abused or refused to work with the gifts given to us–money, time and talent. There needs to arise in all our hearts such a deep desire to PLEASE GOD, to be EFFECTIVE WORKERS IN HIS HARVEST. Think where all of us might be today if He had not stepped down into the mess of our lives and saved us FOR HIMSELF. Jesus told his disciples that the time was so late, He had to work while it was day, for when the night and darkness came, none would be able to work. The window of Obligation and opportunity is quite small in comparison with the wide way of wasting time and talents. Our generation wants to play long, pray short, spend much on self, give hardly nothing into the work of God, make sure the family is taken care of for the future, but do very little to ensure the FUTURE OF THE SOUL.

I know for one that I must get into high–gear quickly; for facing Jesus with anything less than having done my very best is something I do not wish to do. "Where much is known, much is required," the book says and most of us know way more than we are living up to. OUR KNOWLEDGE FAR EXCEEDS OUR OBEDIENCE. We need to develop our faith to new levels.

Our praying must be longer, deeper and richer; yet WITHOUT WORKS, ALL WILL BE IN VAIN. We must yoke up with God. He must do the "for us" and "through us," but we must FILL THE POTS, ROLL AWAY THE STONES, CROSS THE RIVERS, FIGHT THE GIANTS…COME ON, LET'S WORK!

JESUS LEFT HIS WORK TO US, BUT HE'LL BE BACK

We have been given a great honor by Jesus to continue the great work He started, but we must be very aware that HE WILL BE BACK and that we will be forced to face our record. I often shudder at some of the church folks here as I watch them waste their lives on things other than the KINGDOM and SOULS. I wonder if blindness has occurred in some hearts. Jesus has told us to SEEK HIS KINGDOM FIRST, and yet many who read this are doing anything but that. It could be that some of you seek your own personal perception of the work, your own little ideas of what you should put your energies into, but please be reminded that ALL OUR WORK MUST STAND THE FIRE OF GOD AND HIS STANDARD. I would not want to face JESUS with some silly concept that you felt your ways were superior to the BIBLE or to THE LEADERSHIP HE HAS GRANTED YOU.

Moses spent his entire life trying to get the people to listen to him and to comply with instructions he felt they needed. Yet he was constantly resisted by a SEGMENT of folks who always withstood him at every turn. The scary part is revealed in Numbers 14 when Korah and his crew withstood Moses, and God came down to deal with the issue. Moses may have made mistakes, but God felt HE HIMSELF had not when He put the people under the leadership of Moses. In fact, He displayed great wrath unto all who attacked and talked against Moses saying that THEY WERE JUST AS HOLY AND DIDN'T NEED TO OBEY SOME MAN. God was not impressed, and JUDGMENT FELL SWIFTLY. GOD HAS NOT CHANGED. I pray that each of us review our walk with God and our dedication to His work. I pray that we will all ask for a SERVANT'S HEART and strive to spend our lives seeking to save the lost and to build up HIS CHURCH while we can...

THE PROBLEM WITH THE OPINION POLLS IS...

We hear so much today about the opinion polls taken and how much they seem to mean to the stars, the politician and even the CHURCH. SHAME, SHAME, AND MORE SHAME. The only opinion one should be really concerned with is JESUS CHRIST, for if HE is pleased, it really doesn't matter what the public might think of you. The goal in life should be to seek to PLEASE GOD, IMPACT OUR WORLD AND DO EVERYTHING WITHOUT COMPLAINING. Remember that it was Jesus who died to set us free, I must not allow what others might say or think to sidetrack my thinking or actions. It seems like today too many folks are always watching the polls to make sure they are accepted by the masses and not on the wrong side of any issue. The sad part is most of these folks could care less about what GOD THINKS ABOUT THEM...

Paul suffered much because he would not be HELD HOSTAGE by what others said or thought. The driving zeal of his heart remained the same, I MUST HONOR GOD WITH MY LIFE NO MATTER WHO THINKS I AM WRONG OR NARROW-MINDED. You must grasp the fact that the folks who we seem so worried about their opinions, will also go to the JUDGEMENT and answer the LORD about why HIS OPINION didn't matter to them while living on earth. Further more the folks who we seek to be accepted by might die tomorrow, change their opinions like the wind does, or join us later on. WE OUGHT TO OBEY GOD was the reply from the APOSTLES than to allow mere humanity to dictate to us how to live. Please remember to keep your eyes on your exit for we must all face SUNSET some time soon. May GOD help each of us to really seek TO PLEASE GOD FIRST and do all we can to HONOR HIS GOODNESS TO EACH OF US. I want to hear WELL DONE, ENTER THE JOY OF THE LORD.

WHERE IS YOUR FAITH ANYWAY???

I know the Word tells us that God has given to men A MEASURE OF FAITH, but what we do with it is surely within the scope of ourselves. We can use it and help it grow, or we can focus on various things that seem to stunt it or even choke it down to something that is not operative. Faith was the very thing that Jesus looked for among HIS OWN PEOPLE and seemingly could not find much. When He did locate it, HE WOULD ALWAYS COMMEND IT AND REWARD IT. The issue is not DO WE HAVE FAITH, but it is rather, WHERE IS OUR FAITH? We live in a world so blessed with increase in areas of medicine, science, and advancement of every kind. The danger is simple; we can be putting our faith in every place available except in GOD AND HIS TRUTH. We should be so careful not to give away our faith to people, things, or whatever just because it seems best or easier.

During a terrific storm at sea, the men who were in the same boat with Jesus got so afraid, they cried out and asked Him if He even cared about their perishing. He stood up, rebuked the storm, and asked them this question, "WHERE IS YOUR FAITH?" I imagine they could have said, "WHY, IT WAS IN THE ABILITY OF THAT AWFUL STORM TO KILL US." It was in the obvious, the present problem confronting them, the visible, and NOT THE INVISIBLE, OR THE SPIRITUAL. We must seriously fight against putting our faith in things much less than the LORD AND HIS PROMISES. I am not saying not to use what is available or to take advantage of various discoveries, but we must look to the LORD in all things. I know that faith must be tested, that various troubles help build our faith, and that during these times, we are all tempted to leave God out of the situation, trusting all else but Him. We must look to Him in all things.

LORD, OPEN HIS EYES THAT HE MAY SEE

This statement comes from the story of Elisha being surrounded at Dothan and of his young servant, seeing the enemy in power and large numbers, crying out in fear.

I have often been impacted by what Elisha asked, for I think I would have reacted quite differently. I would have asked for God to wipe the enemy out, to send a band of angels and destroy the enemy with one great sweep. Elisha just asks God to please open the servant's eyes, for Elisha and the servant had more for them than against them. Elisha was aware of another world that would take care of the enemy as needed, so he wanted the lad to grasp that truth. Once the servant's eyes were opened to the power standing with them, his fears disappeared, and he knew the victory was assured.

How many times do all of us get so overwhelmed with the obvious things of life and forget the INVISIBLE WORLD? I know God keeps watch over us, and yet at times, life hits me so hard I seem to just wilt and wonder. I am so glad that our GREAT GOD has everything under control, and that NO WEAPON FORMED AGAINST US SHALL PROSPER. I pray for myself often that God would help me to see into the SPIRIT WORLD AND HEAR THAT WORLD. Then I would be able to do so much more for HIM. Why not ask God to open your eyes today, to help you to see and hear the REAL WORLD? I know your fear will diminish, and your FAITH WILL SOAR. I want to see more of what God is doing and wanting to do thru all of us. WITHOUT A VISION, THE PEOPLE PERISH. Ask the Lord to open your eyes and ears to what REALLY MATTERS, WHAT IS THE REAL THING IN LIFE. I believe we all need to see that realm...

OUR PERCEPTIONS ARE PRISONS OR PATHWAYS

I have often heard it said that PERCEPTIONS ARE MUCH GREATER THAN REALITY. In many cases this statement has proven to be very true. I have often had to overcome how I perceived a certain situation before I could really overcome that actual obstacle. Perception can birth within us FEAR. Israel saw the GIANTS AND WALLED CITIES as TOO FORMIDABLE for them to whip. The truth of the matter was quite different; God was going to fight for them and with them. They had just escaped from an impossible prison, EGYPT, walked through the RED SEA, and now their PERCEPTION turns into a PRISON OF DESPAIR AND DEFEAT...

How we perceive any situation, person, or whatever often sends us in a certain direction for victory or defeat. If I feel I can't, I usually cannot. If I sense that somehow I can do it, I usually can.

I read a story regarding the sculptor who did the work on Mount Rushmore. His victory came from his perception of the project. He said, "When everyone else just saw GRANITE UNCARVABLE, I saw four faces struggling to get out. I just chipped away everything that didn't look like the four faces that were in that granite." WOW...I wonder what would happen in our lives, if we could just chip away at everything that is not like the desire we have for something and keep going until that desire is accomplished. THEY SAW ROCK; HE SAW A FINISHED IDEA. May God help all of us to see past the problems, perceiving that in spite of whatever, IF GOD BE FOR US, WHO CAN BE AGAINST US? When God calls us to do something for Him, we must perceive His HELP will be given. We may see ourselves as failures, but God sees our desires and dedication, so He CHIPS AWAY THINGS THAT HINDER US FROM BEING WHAT HE WANTS.

IN HIS GREAT NAME

Jesus gave to the church the grand honor of using HIS NAME to do many things and cause God to be HONORED. I wonder sometimes if we are not really missing what JESUS meant when HE said, "IN MY NAME." We often tack on JESUS' NAME to our prayers and our efforts, and then expect to experience the desired results without really LIVING IN THAT NAME. Naming HIS NAME and LIVING IN HIS NAME are not the same thing. Each revelation we have been given by God should help us to get into an area of revelation by believing and then acting upon what has been revealed. I know I want to LIVE IN HIS NAME. I need to live each day within the various aspects of HIS NAME.

"I will set him on high because he has known my name," says Psalms 91:14. That means more than knowing how to say a name. It must imply total trust. Psalms 9:10 states, "THOSE WHO KNOW YOUR NAME WILL PUT THEIR TRUST IN YOU." Psalms 44:4–5 says, "THROUGH YOUR NAME WE WILL TRAMPLE THOSE WHO RISE UP AGAINST US." It must be more than using His NAME. Matthew 7:21–23 says that many who used HIS NAME will be lost even though miracles occurred while using HIS GREAT NAME. "IN JESUS NAME" has become a sort of tag that insures victory, but I think more is involved than just saying, "IN JESUS NAME."

We need to bathe ourselves into all HIS NAME really reveals–A STRONG TOWER, MY ROCK, THE WAY, THE TRUTH, THE LIFE, THE GOOD SHEPHERD, BREAD OF LIFE, etc. We must HALLOW or SANCTIFY HIS NAME. We must plumb the depth of THAT NAME and allow it to be our pathway through our days.

May God help each of us to live and pray IN JESUS NAME and to walk in the power.

LORD, WHAT WOULD YOU HAVE ME DO?

These words fell from the lips of Saul on the road to Damascus as JESUS stopped his march of harm and terror against the CHRISTIAN CHURCH. Saul now realized he had been totally wrong and that this JESUS did not wish him dead and gone but rather was showing such GREAT MERCY to this once MISTAKEN MAN. Saul felt Jesus had spared him for some purpose yet to be unfolded that Saul wished to know the PLEASURE and PURPOSE of this MERCIFUL JESUS.

Jesus told him to go into the city and it would be revealed to him, what he must do. Interesting, don't you think. Jesus chose not to tell him what to do but rather used a man in the city to do this. Jesus still uses HIS MEN, HIS PREACHERS to give instructions to NEW CONVERTS AND SEASONED SAINTS. Saul gave up his war against the church and now wanted to do whatever this MERCIFUL MESSIAH requested. PLEASING GOD should be as important to us today as it was to SAUL that day, seeing we also have RECEIVED GREAT GRACE AND MERCY. I am very concerned with many who seemingly do not ever want to know HOW TO PLEASE GOD with their lives. SAVED? YES. DESIRE TO REALLY PLEASE GOD IN EVERY WAY? NOT HARDLY. What would make any of us disinterested in the THINGS THAT WOULD PLEASE OUR GOD? Maybe we feel our ways are O.K., or HIS WAYS are too hard, or we just don't care WHAT HE WANTS. I know I want to PLEASE GOD and if I attain everything in life I hope to and yet I have not really pleased God, what will it profit me? Maybe it is time for the body of believers to really start to seek HIS PLEASURE FIRST and everything else will be of little weight. Why not ask the LORD, "WHAT CAN I BE, DO OR WHATEVER, THAT WOULD PLEASE YOU." I know HE WILL ANSWER...

THE CLOUDS ARE
THE DUST OF HIS FEET

The title of this article comes from the Old Testament and carries a grand punch for those of us who live in the New. I have often used this verse showing how God is on His way towards helping us EVEN IN STORMY TIMES. When the prophet Elijah had prayed to end the long draught, his servant saw A CLOUD ARISING from the sea indicating rain was possibly on the way. How often the clouds we are forced to deal with don't look like deliverance or even answers, but rather PROBLEMS AND HINDRANCES that seem to HIDE HIS FACE. Clouds are THE REAL EVIDENCES of the involvement of our God in our behalf, not the activity of our ADVERSARY. Another writer tells us that God would DWELL IN THE THICK DARKNESS, SOMETHING none of us handle too well. I think what the verses are telling us is that God does not always make HIS WAYS CLEAR to us and HE WORKS in situations that seem to appear like disasters. Faithful is He is recorded for our uplifting and so we must view CLOUDY AND DARK situations through the eye of FAITH AND TRUST. While at times we cannot seem to make any sense out of something, God can and will. I cannot tell how long it may take for the Lord to arrive but with just some dust appearing on my horizon I can be assured–HE IS ON THE WAY.

Just in the past few days I have been impacted by some TROUBLING NEWS that seemed to CLOUD UP MY SKIES. Looking anew at the scriptures, it must just be MY FATHER getting ready to do some grand thing in my life. I pray that you also will view YOUR CLOUDS as the DUST OF HIS FEET. HE IS INVOLVED WITH YOU. Remember that a cloud the size of a man's hand brought a harvest to that nation. God loves us somuch. Keep watching those clouds...

I MAY FALL BUT I REFUSE TO STAY DOWN

Sometimes I think many of us FAIL to accomplish many things within our own capacity only because the FEAR OF FAILURE hinders our efforts. I realize that in every venture there is an element of RISK but that very element has the ability to challenge the best within each of us. I cannot afford to be idle or sloppy about something because I COULD FAIL, so what if I FAIL, I AM NOT A FAILURE unless I accept that position. Failing at something that is worthwhile is better than succeeding at another thing that may be MEDIOCRE. I must be willing to CHALLENGE things I know will CHALLENGE ME. THAT IS HOW I LEARN MY LIMITATIONS AND STRENGTHS. "It's hard to beat a person who never gives up." Babe Ruth

You gain strength, courage and confidence by every experience in which you really stop to LOOK FEAR IN THE FACE. "You must do the thing you think YOU CANNOT DO." Roosevelt.

All champions share one rule–they are committed to finish the task, anything less is out of the picture. Success always stops when we do; we must pursue the goal with a determination that borders on CRAZY. I know that things in my life that seemed to hinder me most, hurt me worst, folks who devastated me, have all in the long run been my best BENEFACTORS. Each and every one of us has been helped to our destiny by the episodes that seemed to stop us, but in reality, JUST AS JUDAS was called FRIEND, we too must see OBSTACLES as GOD PLANNED EVENTS to impact us for GOOD. Joseph found the hate of his brothers was actually the hand of God to help him to be and become what the future required.

THE BLESSING OF A DIMINISHED SITUATION

Most of us spend our lives pursuing some object or some goal, and after the chase is over, there seems to be something missing although we have either acquired or accomplished in a certain area. As I sit today looking out the window, I am very restricted in my movements. Many things have been taken away from me yet I feel that I am experiencing an EXPANSION from this time of DIMINISHING. I cannot do various simple things I used to: dress easily, turn quickly, walk without pain, go outside to enjoy nature, yet I am getting a RICHER VIEW of what REALLY MATTERS. I could get angry or depressed over MY CAN'TS but these little losses are allowing my mind to plumb deeper thoughts, perceive principles more clearly, and appreciate the little things in life so that my LOSS has allowed my GAIN. Being forced to sit and not run, to stare and not travel, to be restricted rather than being free has challenged my mind in a very great way. Surely as God washes our eyes with tears so our SOULS can see better, I feel that this time in my life will be a SPRINGBOARD INTO SPIRITUAL THINGS.

Times of loss or diminishing do not have to be the pits; they can be platforms of vision and victory. I know that the many cards and calls I have received have so enriched me, I have been made to feel a warmth from our church family that has not been noticed by me before. Like Elijah of old, I have been set aside for a few days to learn, to grow and become stronger for what lies ahead. May God grant I do not waste MY PAIN or fail to HEAR HIS VOICE. I want to thank all who have prayed for me, for loving me and caring about me. Please ask God to expand the horizon of my spirit during this time, for great things are ahead.

THY PLACE SHALL BE EMPTY, YOU SHALL BE MISSED

The above title comes from the story of David and King Saul. David knows that Saul wishes him much harm, even death so David chooses not to attend a gathering at the palace. He was expected to be there, he had his own chair, so Jonathan tells him THOU SHALT BE MISSED, YOUR PLACE WILL BE EMPTY. I have felt so loved and cared for these past three weeks with the many cards and calls: I HAVE BEEN MISSED. I want to thank all for caring and praying for me. I appreciate being missed but I want to say HOW MUCH I HAVE MISSED MY CHURCH FAMILY. Not being present with fellow believers to worship, to sing songs unto God, to say hello and shake hands, to hug all my little ones and be hugged has taken a great toll on me. I have never missed three weeks of church anytime in my life; I am really overwhelmed by the VOID I have felt in not being with the FAMILY OF GOD.

I must be honest; this situation has challenged my thinking regarding so many that MISS CHURCH for various reasons and think nothing about it. I feel from my position that those who lay out of service, put work or play in front of service, or just don't really care about being there are in very sad shape spiritually. I feel I need to hear the SONGS OF ZION, TO BE AMONG THE REDEEMED, TO GIVE IN THE OFFERING, TO CRY WITH MY CHURCH FAMILY, TO REJOICE WITH THE WORD, TO FEEL GOD TOGETHER. Yes, I have been missed but YOU HAVE BEEN MISSED more by me. I must gather together with you or just dry up and die. The writer of Hebrews told us not to FORSAKE THE ASSEMBLING TOGETHER AS SOME DO. He had much more in mind than we might think. May God bless each of you with a fresh desire to attend regular, to have more input in the services, to worship more and to appreciate the privilege.

IT WAS GOOD FOR ME TO BE AFFLICTED

The above words come to us from the pen of KING DAVID after he had been through a bad time. The pain from his adversity had not been fun but the FOCUS he acquired from it had been more than worth the pain. I feel today that I have been blessed through this little situation in ways I cannot yet fully express but God has been faithful...To be set aside is one thing, but to allow that episode to educate and expand ones vision is quite another. I wonder how many times we waste our problems, pains and setbacks when they could be PLATFORMS for us to see many things MORE CLEARLY. I do not wish trouble upon anyone except within the context of a learning time and growing from it. I know I have a fresh appreciation for God, His Work, People and the gathering together with other folks to worship.

I feel that I have been blessed to take a breather and refocus myself, to weigh some things out a little better and hopefully I can profit from this time of adversity. I know that self-confidence and self-reliance have been given a death blow and that God has allowed me to see; I am NOT NECESSARY for the work to continue, ONLY JESUS IS. I have been made to see how easily some little thing can alter our life, that what we used to do and try can be snatched away so quickly, and that I really do need the body more than I thought I did. My outlook regarding the love and concern from the church family has become so clear; YOU REALLY DO LOVE ME AND CARE ABOUT ME. Thanks to God for the present problems with my health, for it has allowed a FLOW TO HAPPEN that I needed to see and feel. I pray that I can return to the pulpit shortly with a fresh word burning within my soul that can give the direction and inspiration to this body so we can cross over that JORDAN.

FOCUS: THE KEY TO POSSIBILITY

All through the ages God has called to his people, "LOOK UNTO ME" or "BELIEVE MY PROMISES" or "EXPECT THE IMPOSSIBLE." I think the biggest problem for many of us in receiving the SUPERNATURAL is the FOCUS OF OUR VISION, the circumstances, and the obvious. The feelings or absence of those feelings often steal from us the FAITH RELEASE we need to experience the SUPERNATURAL. God gives us various promises to inspire our faith; to create an object for the FOCUS OF OUR FAITH, for He knows life, the devil and the natural instincts will seek to steal from us the ability to expect. To believe and receive one must not only have FAITH; one must have the PROPER OBJECT for our faith. We must SPIRITUALLY STARE OR FOCUS on the PROMISE AND THE ONE WHO HAS PROMISED. The TRIAL OF OUR FAITH is often in this area, the PROMISE IS CLEAR but the PROBLEMS ARE ALSO CLEAR. The OBVIOUS seems to shout so loud to our own UNDERSTANDING, come on and use your common sense, but FAITH must be steadfast, occupied with THE WHO as well as THE WHAT if anything is going to happen. All through history, God has given PROMISES that challenged obvious and natural circumstances but the person who did believe beyond the situation was always rewarded.

HAS GOD PROMISED? HAS HE EVER KEPT HIS WORD TO US BEFORE? IS THERE ANYTHING TOO HARD FOR HIM TO DO? DOES ANOTHER POWER OR PERSON EXIST WHO CAN OVERCOME HIM OR CAUSE HIS WORD TO FAIL? DID HE PROMISE ANYTHING JUST TO CAUSE FRUSTRATION IN OUR FAITH? Once we answer these few questions clearly, it should be easy to expect HIM to keep HIS WORD once again, for HEAVEN AND EARTH SHALL PASS AWAY BUT HIS WORD WILL LAST FOREVER. Ask God to help CLEAR YOUR FOCUS.

INFLUENCE:
DAMAGING OR UPLIFTING

Influence can many times seem to be more impacting than the TRUTH OR FACTS. All through the Bible, TRUTH has often been overcome by some type of influence, either that of some person or perhaps a situation that challenged the TRUTH. In the case of Israel taking the Promised Land, the TRUTH was God had given the land unto them, the FACTS revealed Giants and walled cities, but the entire story revolved around the INFLUENCE OF 12 men who told their stories. Ten said they could not take the land, two said they could. The TRUTH AND FACTS seemed to take a back seat to the POWER OF INFLUENCE. The people disregarded the proof of the fruits, (facts) the promise of God to be with them (truth) the testimonies of all the spies (the land was just like the Lord had said) and their talk and unbelief robbed them of THE PROMISE OF GOD. Influence can really be UPLIFTING OR DAMAGING–what kind are we giving out? Are we allowing the TRUTH OF GOD to challenge obvious FACTS that seem to stand against our FAITH and with our LOOKS, LIPS OR LIVES, INFLUENCE THE WRONG WAY?

Israel had the WORD, THE PROPHETS, THE PRIESTS and yet one nasty gal named JEZEBEL had so much INFLUENCE, she almost wiped out the entire nation. No one seemed to stand up for the TRUTH BUT ALLOWED ERROR TO INFLUENCE THEM INTO DISASTER. Our own country is a story of INFLUENCE, of ideas, concepts and efforts, for INFLUENCE can override what is right at times–consider the rate of crime and drug scene today. TRUTH AND FACT shout to this generation–DON'T DO THAT! DISASTER AND DEATH AWAIT YOU, but through INFLUENCE of TV, VIDEO, PEER PRESSURE AND THE MEDIA, the TRUTH AND FACTS TAKE A BACK SEAT. May God help each of us to become INFLUENCERS FOR THE KINGDOM OF GOD, THE SOULS OF MANKIND and OUR OWN WELL BEING.

THE PARADE AND THE PRAISE

This weekend we celebrate the Fourth of July: INDEPENDENCE DAY from the bad treatment we had been getting from our former homeland. It took a great deal of courage in that day to make the BREAK with England, knowing full well an attack and suffering would be shortly coming. Yet these brave souls felt the price to be paid was well worth the blessing of being totally free. We usually remember that grand day with some type of parade, a day off from work, hot dogs and fireworks. I am wondering if we will offer God some real PRAISE for what was done for the human race when JESUS died for the SOULS of mankind. CALVARY AND PENTECOST must be the two grand dates on the calendar of heaven. One, man was purchased and on the other, man would be filled. Free and filled, what more could God offer to any of us.

Sometimes I fear that we who have been FREED AND FILLED have not counted on the FIERCE FOE aiming his guns at us and seeking to take us back as his property. Maybe we should think this thing out a bit more, like our forefathers did at our SIGNING THAT DECLARATION OF INDEPENDENCE. When we REPENT and are BAPTIZED God steps in and WASHES, CLEANSES AND FORGETS all our past. When we receive the HOLY GHOST God moves into the HOUSE HE PURCHASED and begins to set up our lives in line with HIS PURPOSE. We must EXPECT the devil to try and RECAPTURE us, or at least mess with our lives so we are discouraged often. I think we need to fill our mouths with PRAISE AND THANKSGIVING more than we do for this weapon will deter our adversary from any MAJOR VICTORIES in our lives.

HIS WAYS ARE PAST FINDING OUT!

If you have tried walking with the LORD for any length of time you will have to agree with me, HIS WAYS ARE PAST FINDING OUT. God seems to do some seemingly strange things in the life of a believer, things that seem to cause questions rather than robust faith. The WHY of many things can be very upsetting to say the least, especially when you feel your heart is right and your desire seems to be for HIS WORK. I wonder if PAUL didn't wonder at why he had been put out of circulation with his often prison stays. He wanted to be OUT THERE doing what he had been called to do, yet God seemed to enjoy taking him apart sometimes to do some other work. I think we all need to look at what God seems to take us from and then put us into and ask, WHY AM I HERE AND WHAT DOES HE WANT ME TO DO NOW? Being laid aside does not mean CAST ASIDE, it means that we are in need of some STILLNESS, SOME THERAPY, SOME DEEPER THOUGHT, SOME REST, BOTH SPIRITUAL AND PHYSICAL. Our VISION can be helped much when we are forced into something we didn't want and must deal with it.

I am sure ELIJAH was perplexed when God sent him to sit by that DRYING BROOK when his heart burned to be doing something. I know that God was preparing him for a much greater future because I have read the whole story. I know that my past 8 weeks of rehab have been deeply impacting, on my desires to do and yearning to be. I know MY TIMES ARE IN HIS HANDS so this time too has been ORDERED OF THE LORD. I pray that each of us can learn from our DOWN TIMES and allow them to be UP TIMES, LEARNING AND GROWING TIMES.

THY WORD IS FOREVER SETTLED IN HEAVEN

There is nothing in this world more powerful than the WORD OF GOD, for it is the actual THOUGHT, DESIRE, INTENT AND WISHES of the CREATOR HIMSELF. The Bible tells us that God caused the cosmos to become visible with the BREATH OF HIS MOUTH. Just with His Word He caused life to be, things to be formed, laws to step into place and seasons to continue. In Psalms it tells us ANGELS do their work according to the VOICE OF HIS WORD, not ours. One writer tells us, HEAVEN AND EARTH SHALL PASS AWAY BUT THY WORD WILL NOT PASS AWAY.

The WORD OF GOD is none other than God telling all of us HIS WILL, HIS WAYS and HIS THOUGHTS. No wonder JESUS was and is the WORD OF GOD manifested in flesh, the actual thoughts and purpose of God made VISIBLE. He told us that to see HIM was the same as seeing the FATHER, FOR HE AND THE FATHER WERE ONE. The only division within the GODHEAD is that of SPIRIT AND FLESH, NOT PERSONS. God is SPIRIT and that SPIRIT BECAME FLESH so that a SACRIFICE with BLOOD could be made, for God didn't have any BLOOD TO SHED until He became a man.

There seems to be a general disregard today regarding the WORD as if it was some type of HISTORICAL OPINION that can be disregarded at will. Jesus warned all mankind that we would be JUDGED by THE WORD, not someone's idea about it. When God opens HIS MOUTH and speaks, God means what He says, and all the universe stands to attention. That is, EXCEPT MANKIND. What a tragedy that we can be so smart about some things and yet totally ignorant about the ETERNAL WORD OF GOD that will someday JUDGE OUR VERY SOULS. Our entire FUTURE will flow from the position we take with regard to WHAT HAS BEEN WRITTEN. May God grant us MERCY to take into our hearts HIS EVERLASTING WORD and do all we can to comply and conform to it by the GRACE OF GOD. Remember; HIS WORD CANNOT BE BROKEN. It may be VIOLATED, IGNORED, ATTACKED; BUT IT LIVES.

IF GOD BE FOR US, HOW CAN WE LOSE

How often have we heard or read this great statement and yet found it so hard to really accept it as a working fact in our lives. I know for myself, that when I have failed in some area, I don't feel at that time GOD IS FOR ME. The truth of the matter is, when we have stumbled or failed, HIS GRACE and MERCY are flowing towards us like a great river. Even as we love and care for our own children when they have gone through some mess, seeking to assure them that it will be OK, God also sends HIS WORD OUR WAY. Our FEELINGS hinder our FAITH in HIS WORD; thus we have OUR TRIAL OF OUR FAITH.

The THRONE OF GRACE beckons to us most when we are in the TIME OF NEED, believe this with all your heart. God does not diminish HIS LOVE for us over our sins, for HIS BLOOD was shed for those sins. He knew what we would do when He saved us. Calvary was for us, the Blood was for us, His praying was for us, the Holy Ghost is for us, the PLACE CALLED HEAVEN is for us, the ANGELS are working with and for us. BE ENCOURAGED CHILD OF GOD. I am so glad God is for me; that transfigures every episode, every trial, every time I falter. GOD IS FOR ME. He loves me so much, he allows me to reach the end of my ability and strength so I can fall back upon HIS GRACE AND POWER. I must believe this truth or FRUSTRATE HIS GRACE in my life. I am not in this race by myself, God has ordered my steps. He is seeking my growth and victory more than I am. Paul told us that we should be to THE PRAISE OF HIS GLORY; He seeks to get honor from our lives.

May God lift your eyes towards that THRONE OF GRACE in time of need. THE WELCOME MAT IS STILL OUT…

SALVATION—BOTH GREAT AND BEAUTIFUL

The word tells us that God would beautify the MEEK with salvation. He would grant an ENHANCING OF BEAUTY to those who would be meek. It seems to me that our salvation would have to be a THING OF BEAUTY and not some UGLY something that so many seem to say about it. Anything that God works with usually will become much nicer and better than when it, or they, had been left alone. God is always lifting, changing, improving everything He works with; for God is a God of the BEST, THE BEAUTIFUL. To Him, the status of anything He begins with doesn't seem to matter. After all, He is ALMIGHTY and able to alter anything. I am so glad for our BEAUTIFUL SALVATION that is offered to any and all. God alone can lift from the gutter, from sin and shame and transform us into a thing of beauty, for He is the God of all Grace.

His call unto us to be HOLY is not a thing of ugliness but of beauty, to be LIKE HIM in all our ways is both grand and glorious to say the least. To think that God wants us back from sin and brought into a place in HIM is grand to say the least. To see folks who have wasted their lives in sin be brought to the CROSS, to the WATER and to the POWER OF PENTECOST, is just fantastic.

Salvation is also GREAT. For the power of sin is broken, the power of an endless life is brought into our bodies by the HOLY GHOST. To think that we can be the HOUSE OF GOD, HIS TEMPLE, and to have the past erased by HIS PRECIOUS BLOOD, is nothing short of GREAT. Our God is GREAT, HIS SALVATION PLAN IS GREAT and HIS MERCY TOWARDS US IS GREAT and finally, HIS FAITHFULNESS IS TOTALLY GREAT. He that has begun a GOOD WORK in us will bring it to a finish for HIS GLORY AND OUR BENEFIT.

THE GOD OF ALL RESTORATION WORK

Most of this church family knows how much I have enjoyed RESTORING OLD CARS but maybe you have not known the WHY. I have so enjoyed the fact that something could be taken back to the ORIGINAL STATE with some hard work and investment. I have received so many messages from this hobby, thoughts that have been spiritual. The God we serve surely is the first and foremost RESTORER and He alone knows just what the particular object should be like. In the beginning, God moved on the earth to RESTORE IT, the same is true regarding MANKIND. Something was created then ruined, then God stepped on the scene to RESTORE BACK TO THE ORIGINAL.

I am so glad God loves to RESTORE PEOPLE to HIS ORIGINAL PLAN for their lives, not hauling humanity off to the JUNKYARD. I know He has put many hours into our lives working with patience and purpose to get all of us back to HIS ORIGINAL DESIGN. I have been involved with completing a car and once it was done, I felt both a sense of achievement and then a kind of funny emptiness. I think that the real fun was the effort to do it rather than the final finished product. I know from various compliments I have received at shows, the work done to the cars affected other folks and that brought me a sense of joy.

I am sure as God works His GREAT RESTORATION in our lives, the finished, or at least the GREAT IMPROVEMENT that is seen, affords HIM GREAT JOY. It takes a lot of effort and money to accomplish some things, especially when the product one is now laboring with was a BASKET CASE. God is so POWERFUL, PATIENT AND WELL FIXED, HE can take the worst and make them FANTASTIC. May God help each of us to get involved with Him in the RESTORATION WORK…

THERE IS NO SUBSTITUTE FOR THE TRUTH

The world in which you and I live has become a literal cesspool of lies and falsehood. The God of Glory knew it would be like this, and in HIS GREAT WISDOM He allowed us to be part of this situation. The DECEIVER has been working hard to keep the minds and souls of the lost in the dark about what really matters. I know OUR GREAT LORD JESUS told us to obey the truth, love the truth and that the TRUTH would set us free. Free from what you might ask? Free from the SHAME that living a lie will give you, free from living with GUILT, free from SLEEPLESS NIGHTS OF FEAR. I read this one time and I think it sure is worth repeating: "LIVE THE TRUTH INSTEAD OF POSSESSING IT, TELL THE TRUTH AND YOU WON'T HAVE TO TRY TO REMEMBER WHAT YOU SAID."

TRUTH today is what is needed, in every aspect of life, for it alone can and will SET US FREE. We must KNOW WHAT WE BELIEVE and then WE WILL KNOW WHAT TO DO. The world we are a part of is constantly seeking to squeeze us into the mold but we must RESIST AND REFUSE. The fact that certain practices and life-styles have been made the ACCEPTABLE NORM has come too late for me; FOR JESUS, HIS LIFE AND WORDS, alone has become the STANDARD for my life. He was and is the PERFECT MODEL and we should strive to die out to ourselves and allow HIS NATURE AND WILL to direct all our ways. This world always measures the HEAD but God measures OUR HEARTS and that is really what counts. It is not so much the DEEDS done that count but rather THE WHY, the MOTIVES that matter the most. REMEMBER, the person who would lead the orchestra, must turn their back to the crowd. BUY THE TRUTH AND SELL IT NOT STILL WORKS!

A GREAT DIFFERENCE: TO GLANCE OR GAZE

When the people of Israel were in trouble from being bitten by serpents, they were told that EVERYONE THAT LOOKETH SHALL LIVE. Life for just a LOOK, but what kind of looking did God intend? I must tell you there is quite a difference between a casual glance and a deep gaze. Things we just glance at become much more understandable when we begin to GAZE at them. The gaze allows many things to be seen that through a glance were hidden. To gaze is really TO BEHOLD ATTENTIVELY, which explains why SIGHT IS A GIFT BUT SEEING IS AN ART. How many folks can see what another totally misses, and yet both are looking at the same thing. How many today glance at the CHRIST AND THE CROSS and miss everything. But those who will GAZE are so moved with what they behold, they begin to repent. To STARE INTENTLY AT HIS BLEEDING BODY will cause us to grasp the fact; THIS IS WHAT MY SIN HAS DONE TO HIM. That real intense gazing will allow the SWORD OF TRUTH to cut deep into our innermost being and cause us to pour out our hearts in THANKSGIVING for JESUS taking our place.

I read a line once that stated something terrible yet true: WHEN ONE REALLY SEES JESUS ON THE CROSS, IT CAUSES DEATH TO EVERY VICE. It is while we GAZE at the CROSS that we begin to LOATHE OUR SINS and seek TO ADMIT THEM AND THEN QUIT THEM. He died that we might live but we too must DIE SO THAT HE MAY LIVE WITHIN US and this must flow from a DEEP GAZING and not some SHALLOW GLANCE. WE ARE ONLY PROMISED LIFE WHEN WE REALLY TAKE TIME AND LOOK DEEPLY.

STOP GLANCING–START GAZING

EXCEPT IT DIE–BUT IF IT DIE

Jesus had been teaching the truth of how a harvest required the death of a seed thus showing HIS OWN DEATH soon to be accomplished. In life, we often view DEATH OR DYING as some terrible thing, but to God IT IS A MUST if the PERFECT WILL OF GOD is to be accomplished. Jesus said, if the seed does not die, it remains alone. The HARVEST cannot occur because the LIFE WITHIN THE SEED cannot come forth while still contained in the shell. The LIFE must be allowed to come breaking forth so a HARVEST will happen, thus showing DEATH IS NOT DEFEAT, but rather a STEP NEEDED. Man fell into sin and died. The LORD JESUS thus had to die and fall into the ground so man can experience SPIRIT LIFE. While Jesus died ALONE for the sins of the world, when HE AROSE, HE CAME WITH MANY OTHERS, the fruits of HIS DYING.

The truth is obvious; if we are to be FRUITFUL in life, we must die to SIN AND SELF. If we spend our lives living for ourselves, WE LIVE IN VAIN. If we are willing to LOSE OUR LIVES in HIS SERVICE, we are told, we will KEEP THEM UNTO LIFE ETERNAL. If we are not willing to DIE OUT TO OURSELVES, our efforts at self–preservation will fail and we will have WASTED OUR LIVES. What a great blessing to have our lives dedicated to God to such a place that through our dying to self and sin, God is willing to use that as the SEED FOR A GREAT HARVEST.

May God help each of us to be willing to die out to anything that might hinder HIS PURPOSE for our lives so we can be used for a MIGHTY MULTIPLIED HARVEST.

DREAMS DO COME TRUE WITH GOD

The Lord has been visiting our church services in a grand way and we are so thankful. Sometimes it really seems like a dream, a wish longed for or maybe just a deep hope within our hearts to see the Lord working in us and for us. It sure does seem like a TIME of REFRESHING from HEAVEN and a DREAM COME TRUE.

I am so glad about all that have been BAPTIZED of late and the number of souls filled with the HOLY GHOST. The Jews spoke of the time when their God turned their captivity, it seemed like a dream come true. I feel the same way right now. It seems we've been in a long trying, waiting period with the new church building, but they are now ready to pour the slab and the steel should be going up within a week or two.

The altar services of late have been wonderful. I am thrilled with the way so many of you have just stepped into MINISTRY to help seekers. Please continue to do so, for once we all were lost, needing God and someone helped us to pray and to walk with the Lord. So please keep up the good work!

Our fresh focus in FASTING AND PRAYER will surely bring some wonderful results, not only in the area of FUTURE HARVEST OF SOULS but also in our own GROWTH AND MATURITY. Some things can only be accomplished in this manner, so please find your day to fast, stick to it and watch God HONOR OUR EFFORTS.

As we face this new year, let each one purpose to be more like Jesus, bringing each area of our lives into alignment with HIS WILL. I know that God wants to bless us, so be honest about CHANGING, SEEKING GOD and becoming PASSIONATE ABOUT SPIRITUAL THINGS.

THE POWER OF THE ALTAR

I thank God for His wonderful idea called the ALTAR–a meeting place where man can approach his God and offer unto Him a SACRIFICE, a PRAISE, a PRAYER for help and a CHANCE to COMMUNICATE with GOD. God has always told mankind that we could not just approach Him except via an altar where blood was spilled or confession was offered. Jesus told us that when we came to the ALTAR, if we remember that someone has something against us, we must leave our gift there and be reconciled to him or her, then return to the altar and offer our gift. It is the ALTAR that sanctifies our gifts; the ALTAR has power to remind us of various wrongs that must be made right. An ALTAR reveals to us that we are far from perfect and that our God is waiting and willing to deal with us in MERCY. The ALTAR is a place to do serious business with God, to repent, to receive the SPIRIT, to confess our faults, to be reconciled to God and others.

After Abraham failed in Egypt, he went back to his first altar and there he sacrificed and talked with his God. It must have been such a relief to his soul to be back in the place where he could pour out his failures and feelings to his father. THANK God for ALTARS ALONG the JOURNEY of LIFE that have HELPED US ALL. An auditorium without an ALTAR is still just an auditorium. The presence of an ALTAR makes it a MEETING PLACE, not the furniture, the carpet or instruments. It has the power to alter any situation and is so easy to erect, just open your heart freely and offer yourself to HIM. We may have a program, a plan, etc., but the ALTAR allows us to meet God and be impacted.

KEEP AN ALTAR IN YOUR LIFE.

THERE IS A PLACE BY ME FOR YOU

I have often read this wonderful truth that God had spoken to Moses when he desired to behold THE GLORY of GOD. I think it is quite interesting that this request came from a REDEEMED MAN who had seen God do amazing things both in Egypt and in Israel's walk from slavery through the wilderness. There was something alive in Moses that seemed to say, THANKS FOR THE PAST, BUT I KNOW YOU ARE MUCH GREATER THAN WHAT I HAVE TASTED SO FAR. I too have had this inner longing to step into the next level in God, whatever that may be and no matter the cost involved. God has been so grand to each of us, but I feel the time has come for this assembly to become hungry for the GLORY OF GOD like we have never been to date.

I know many of you want to know God better, understand more of HIS WAYS, learn how to Walk and live in the SPIRIT and to be all that He wants you to be. I am firmly convinced that none of these will occur for any of us without a real HUNGER and THIRST flowing from within our SPIRITS. God desires to be SOUGHT AFTER. His offers are true, but seeking their workings in our lives surely rests with us. I personally want to find that place near Him: a place where I can rise above the norm of average church life and learn of Him. I know for Moses that it surely meant He had to leave many people behind as he climbed up to that place.

A great effort was made to climb that high and sacrifice was required. Are we willing to ascend ALONE? Willing to leave behind whatever in order to find that PLACE by HIM? Keep up your fasting and prayer. Ask for a fresh hunger from HIM for HIM. He is always pleased with honest seekers and promises to be found by any and all who seek whole heartedly.

GRANT US BOLDNESS

This prayer from the early church must once again become our heart beat and desire. It is very important what we believe, WHO we believe in but most of all, that HIS POWER flows through our lives to the depth that we can accomplish what HE wants us to do. I know that the early believers had seen Jesus in action. This surely gave them the faith that what HE had done in their presence, HE could and would do again. They knew they were not able in any way to impact their world with the ability they had nor with a story they wished to relate. They were so aware that it would take HIS POWER WORKING 'in them' to convince their hearers and set captives free. Their boldness could only flow from the assurance that HE would allow them to be touched with the SUPERNATURAL.

I am praying that this church will first pray for the power of God to operate in our lives to the level that we will not be intimidated or afraid to witness and speak. Ask God to help me to speak the WORD with AUTHORITY, COMPASSION AND CONVICTION, for the PULPIT must lead this church. Then ask the LORD to empower you with fervor and intensity to step out into the work for Him.

I know I have often spoken about being bolder but the NEED IS SO GREAT and the TIME IS SO SHORT. Won't you seek HIS FACE? I believe God is waiting for us to cry out to Him for this blessing. Join Me Now.

THE BEST POSITION OF THE SOUL STRONG

In Acts 27, Paul is in a horrible storm at sea, all hope seems to be gone and he tells the disciples, "don't be afraid, I BELIEVE GOD, IT WILL BE LIKE I WAS TOLD. TO BELIEVE GOD is the finest position for any person to take, no matter how terrible the existing situation might be. When we REALLY BELIEVE GOD we do not take our cues from the storms of life, the balance on our bank account, or the test results at the hospital. For WITH GOD ALL THINGS ARE POSSIBLE. I think all of us are attacked by our enemy by various events in life, each one trying its very best to steal our PEACE and JOY.

To be a true believer is not a little thing, for the world, the devil, the flesh, our past, our families and friends are usually challenging our STAND OR FAITH. Many times we are forced to stand totally alone even from other believers and this usually is quite a tough stand to take. I know that FAITH PLEASES GOD so it must surely ANNOY the ADVERSARY, that is surely why Paul said, "we are not ignorant of his devises." Sometimes we are asked to believe God when there seems to be no reason or good explanation but FAITH GOES FAR BEYOND OUR HUMAN UNDERSTANDING and lays hold of the resources and power of another world from which this present world came from.

May God grant each of us the desire to reach into the SPIRIT REALM and be convinced that God will not fail anyone of us and that HE has great plans for the BELIEVER.

LOOK ON THE FIELDS, LOOK UNTO THE HILLS

Jesus told his disciples to look on the fields for they were already WHITE to HARVEST. He then told them to PRAY for the Lord of the HARVEST to send workers into the HARVEST. I feel that the sequence is very important. We must view the HARVEST that SHOWS the REASON for OUR BEING in HIS GREAT KINGDOM, and grants each of us a wonderful job description. The size of the HARVEST and the readiness of it must cause us to LOOK UNTO THE HILLS for the help needed. I feel the first LOOK should be the driving force into the second LOOK, realizing that we cannot do the job that is waiting on us unless GOD HELPS US.

Our VISION will always determine our VICTORY. I must behold my mission and then behold the LORD OF THAT MISSION. If I am unmoved by the HARVEST committed to me, I surely will not lift my eyes any higher than my little world. God did not seek and save any of us just so we could enjoy His great blessings, be secure with the promise of a glorious future and to miss hell. He touched each of us so we could be sent back into the field and seek others to be spared for HIS NAMESAKE.

We must ask ourselves some tough questions. What is my job here? Am I doing anything to expand His kingdom? Do I care about the lost? We are STEWARDS unto God for the truths He has given to us. We must seek to share this wonderful message of mercy with others. I pray that our eyes will behold the HARVEST and the HEAVENS from whence comes our help. Look on, Look unto and Look for His GREAT Appearing. May God help each of us.

THE BLESSING OF TAKING A RISK

I read an article a little while ago that contained a wonderful truth, IT IS A GREAT MISTAKE IN LIFE TO TAKE THE SAFE PATH. How many times do we all want to take the SAFE PATH or the way of LEAST RESISTANCE. Not too many people enjoy CONFRONTATION, HARDSHIP or TOUGH THINGS. We all seem to delight in staying in the SAFETY ZONES or COMFORT ZONES which seem to afford us living without the pain of RISKING.

Yet RISK is just another way of spelling FAITH. The act of getting beyond the SHORE. To experience and explore the OCEAN. Horizons are not just for the looking and talking about. They seem to beckon to the deep within all of us. It takes a lot of courage to leave the tested, tried and secure areas of life to experience the unknown and uncharted. Yet this is exactly what we are called to do. We MUST STEP OUT OF THE BOAT TO WALK ON THE WATER. Without stepping beyond the SECURE we can never realize the potential that God has put down inside each of us nor will we ever become all God has designed us to be. The FEAR of the new, different or the unusual have for years held many hostage and left them to walk the SAFE PATH

As a boy I heard this often, "Better safe than sorry." Sometimes staying safe in SPIRITUAL THINGS can leave us more SORRY THAN SAFE. Regret is a tough thing to live with. Living life without TAKING A RISK can be a real bummer. The leaving of the SAFE PATH is not easy. GREAT COURAGE is often needed and will be granted upon request. God Has promised!

May God grant each of us the desire and courage to launch out into a fresh direction and walk on that thing that is scary right now.

THE WIND IS BLOWING AGAIN

Years ago, we enjoyed the Wolfe Trio singing a song by that title, but today we are forced to deal with weird winds of doctrine that are blowing once again. Our generation has gone on record that DOCTRINE is of little interest or even consequence, but I beg to differ. We have been warned again and again in the Bible about the Winds of Doctrine that would be blowing in the END TIMES. I can read the paper, listen to the radio or just talk with people and realize that the WIND is BLOWING AGAIN. If a wind is strong enough, it can blow the best ship off course or even cause that vessel to become shipwrecked. The enemy of our souls is using the MEDIA, WORLDLY CHURCH, CARNAL BELIEVERS, and THE PASSION FOR PLEASURE and FUN to blow the church off course. We must realize that the wind that we are facing has an intention of destruction and defeat. The wind can also cause a ship to be delayed, or slowed down to a crawl so that the original purpose for the sailing is totally lost.

Paul warned us not to be carried about with EVERY WIND of DOCTRINE. We must get on OUR KNEES and into HIS WORD so we can know what is correct and will be able to resist ERROR and EVIL. As I listen to the church world a shiver goes down my back because I sense such great deception. It is now blowing into the REAL CHURCH of JESUS CHRIST. Folks, believe me this is no time to be caught off guard, nor to entertain breezes blowing your way that whisper, IT DOESN'T MATTER, JUST BELIEVE.

We must believe right, live right, and be right if we plan to end up RIGHT.

WE MUST HAVE SOUND DOCTRINE

Our day seems to be one of tolerance and hazy thinking in regards to the spirit life of humanity. I am quite concerned about the slant of society towards the idea that only in the world of religion, exactness, specifics, and correctness does not really matter. In science, medicine, construction, and every other area of human thought and effort, ACCURACY IS DEMANDED. When mankind deals with physical things he surely demands total unerring truth, but dealing with the SPIRITUAL and ETERNAL, he now takes a position that TRUTH DOES NOT MATTER, BEING REPLACED WITH SINCERITY.

Right thinking about spiritual matters is imperative to right living, for our doctrines of life help develop our thinking and acting. SOUND CHARACTER DOES REQUIRE SOUND TEACHING AND DOCTRINE. The Lord Jesus was very definite about what He wanted His followers to expound and live out as His witnesses. Our day of anything goes will cause many to be lost. We must adhere to APOSTOLIC DOCTRINE and EXAMPLES. Moral power has always flowed from beliefs that were Godly. The great saints of the past were always dogmatic in precept, which produced practices that honored God and blessed mankind.

The early church not only taught truth but they also contended for its purity. I am pleading with all of you to contend for the faith once delivered to the saints, for it can save you and those who hear you. IT DOES MATTER WHAT WE BELIEVE.

BE NOT WEARY IN WELL DOING

Be not weary in well doing–this challenging writing comes to us from the pen of Paul, or should I say HIS SOUL. If anyone should have, or could have had reason to be WEARY in WELL DOING, it was Paul. He put his life on the line over and over to help others, often denying himself the very basics of life so he would not be a burden to others. This statement is much easier to read or quote than it is to live out for we all get WEARY DOING WELL while we get the short end of the stick, as it were. Being taken advantage of, or just being overlooked or not being thanked sometimes can be quite a load to carry. The rest of the verse tells us that IN DUE SEASON WE SHALL REAP, IF WE DON'T FAINT. There is a God above who alone controls the seasons, and He has promised, IN DUE SEASON, reaping will occur if we don't faint.

Our enemy seeks constantly to get us frustrated, sidetracked, anxious and just plain WEARY with it all. He can't force anyone to do wrong or quit, but by wearing us down, or showing us the hopelessness of any situation, WE WILL CHOOSE TO QUIT. He can't separate us from the LOVE OF GOD but at different times we have our own doubts about God's love for us. He that endures unto the end shall be saved, that settles it for me.

I read the following the other day and it grabbed me totally. May you be impacted too: A MAN IS NOT FINISHED WHEN HE IS DEFEATED, HE IS FINISHED WHEN HE QUITS.

Keep trying, praying, praising, witnessing, for God is aware and will reward each of us at the DUE SEASON.

FOR THE JOY THAT WAS SET BEFORE ENDURED

This portion of the WORD comes to us from Hebrews, telling us of the power of determination and vision. Jesus had to face the horror of mistreatment, beatings, injustice and shame, finally the cruelty of the cross, yet He endured. How? He saw the joy that followed the cross, the saving of our souls, the filling of the Holy Ghost, His returning to get His Church. These things helped to give him the power to ENDURE THE CROSS, even though He despised the shame. Is it not wrong to dislike, feel bad about, and actually draw back from certain distasteful things as long as we finish our task? We, like Jesus must look beyond the present struggles and problems to the victory that has been promised to us by the one who died for us long ago. He surely knows how we all feel when faced with various things in life that seem so terrible. But, He has promised grace and power to do His will.

I know that I talk and write quite often about vision, but it really impacts so many areas of our lives. We must look beyond the obvious and present, believing that He will not allow anything into our lives that would of itself destroy, defeat or divorce us from fulfilling His will. God is too faithful to play games with our hearts and souls. He loves us too much to be happy over our fears and hurts. Faithful is he who has called us, who will also bring it to pass. This must be written deep within our spirits.

Pray for joy that can see beyond the tears and knows that the sun will shine again. I pray you will look beyond, for without that vision, you won't go beyond the present.

THE TRIAL OF YOUR FAITH IS PRECIOUS

No one really enjoys any type of trouble or pressure, yet in the economy of God pressures, trials, and problems play such an important part. God requires that our lives and faith be tried and challenged. He knows that a faith untested cannot be trusted, nor will it ever accomplish what He desires it to.

All of those listed in Hebrews 11 are shown through their different trials and episodes that gave Glory to God and let the tried be blessed and matured. Each of them seemingly was tested in various ways and, at the time, the trial seemed totally horrendous. God has shown Himself faithful and caring over and over again. Since He cannot change, we can know that we will come through whatever testing and trials God has sent our way. We need to understand that our testing is both a vote from God for us and an avenue by which we will reveal the wonder of His grace. He knows just how much we can take, and how much needs to be taken from us, so we can become as pure gold. When the various alloys are removed from gold by the fire process, the value of purified gold is much greater. The trials we are put through are designed to purify our faith and our being, so the end result will be a believer of great value.

May the Lord give each of us the determination and desire to be what he wants and the willingness to yield ourselves to things we cannot even grasp at the time. The fiery furnace gave us the story of the three Hebrew boys and the lion's den revealed Daniel to us. I'm sure none of them wanted the way they were forced to go. Trials are opportunities from God to honor Him, prove the devil a liar, and show this world God is Good Always.

THE REAL PURPOSE OF PRESSURE

I am sure that all who will read this little article can relate to living under pressure and the feeling of frustration that often comes with it. Pressure is not our enemy, but rather a revealer of what we are made of, what really matters to us and various areas in our lives that need some more work. I know that pressure has been a blessing to me, even though at the time I didn't appreciate the problem. I have found out that I often can operate at a higher level of accomplishment through being under that pressure.

It seems to call latent ability from within me and also allows my very being to open up to the TOUCH OF GOD. The pressure of Jacob regarding the coming of Esau caused him to seek God and plead promises that were given long before the present pressure arrived. Pressure seems to jog our memory with regard to the things of God that we often forget about. The pressure put on Joseph's brothers caused them to recall their terrible crime and allowed forgiveness to flow into their lives. Pressure will either make us into better people or bitter people, but for sure, pressure won't allow us to stay the way it first found us. Peter told us that the TRIAL OF OUR FAITH WAS BY FIRE, so the process was for our purifying that we would be more like the Lord wanted us to be. I must not curse that pressure, but allow it to purge me, purify me and reveal things in me that must change, AMEN. A diamond is simply a piece of coal that stayed true under pressure. Let's do the same for His name and glory.

PERSPECTIVE IS SO POWERFUL

It all depends on how you "see things" we've been told from our childhood, and it sure seems to be grand advice. Any situation can be viewed numerous ways, and our PERSPECTIVE AND FOCUS of that situation is much more impacting and powerful than the situation itself. Job could have allowed the various episodes that occurred to him to absolutely drive him to despair and failure, but he had a good perspective. WHAT WAS IT? THE LORD WAS AND IS ALWAYS IN CHARGE OF ALL AND ANY SITUATION REGARDLESS OF PAIN, LOSS, OR MYSTERY. The Lord Reigns–let the earth rejoice.

I feel that to focus spiritually in each situation is really a great TRIAL OF OUR FAITH. It seems so easy to react carnally and go to scrapping and lowering oneself to fight it out. I know from my own failures in these things that what I am saying is true, but to live them out when under strain and pressure, well, that is a different story altogether. Ha! Ha!

Of late, I have been feeling the hot fires of being REFINED and PURIFIED. While I do not like them at all, I have taken refuge in the fact, THAT THE REFINER IS MY FATHER. He alone knows what impurities remain inside of my being, and what heat will be required to burn them out. May God help each one of us to realize that trouble does not mean we have failed God, nor are we being rebellious, but rather we are being PROCESSED and when we are tried, we shall come forth as PURE GOLD

Though we may despise the problems, may God grant us PROPER PERSPECTIVE so we can rest in HIS HANDS.

MY THANKS TO HIM AND TO HIS CHURCH

Today my heart is overflowing with THANKS to God for all He has allowed me to experience and express, regarding HIS WORK AND HIS PEOPLE. This past weekend was a grand time for this body and TO GOD BE THE GLORY. I am so very glad for HIS CHURCH AND FOR THIS CHURCH; for I know from the Bible, the CHURCH IS HIS VEHICLE FOR EXPRESSING HIS WILL. I am glad to be a part of this local assembly; for it has afforded me the opportunity to contribute, to learn and to be blessed in so doing. I know that some today may feel the CHURCH is a piece of JUNK, A PROBLEM, A PLACE THAT TAKES FOLKS MONEY, STEALS THEIR TIME AND REALLY should be done away with. I stand against all the SELF–APPOINTED CRITICS, for God has said HE WOULD BUILD HIS CHURCH and so I will continue to WORK WITH HIM.

I know of no other institution on earth that God so loves, works within, and seeks to assist like the CHURCH. I would not want to blame it, blast it, steal from it, seek to avoid it and surely never offer it SECOND BEST OR LEFTOVERS. I know that someday God will LIFT IT OFF the earth, that the BOOKS WILL BE OPEN. ALL THE TRUTH WILL BE TOLD AND EVERY EFFORT, OR LACK OF EFFORT WILL BE REVEALED. THE LORD WILL REWARD THE LOYAL, THE FAITHFUL, THE COMMITTED, and then it will be worth everything to HAVE DONE EVERYTHING for HIS CHURCH AND OUR LOCAL CHURCH. May God work with us to AWAKEN WITHIN US A BURNING DESIRE TO BE DEDICATED AND LOYAL; for the time is short.

Don't live your life for anything less than what God is working with and for. Love the CHURCH.

ACCEPT NO SUBSTITUTES

I have often read the above line with regard to certain items for sale, for items that were supposed originals, and I feel all through the SCRIPTURES, the same call comes. Whatever you do with regard to DOCTRINE, EXPERIENCES AND TRUTH; ACCEPT NO SUBSTITUTES, FOR THESE THINGS WILL AFFECT YOUR ETERNAL DESTINY. I feel compelled to warn all who read this; THE DEVIL OF DECEPTION is working full throttle and would like nothing better than to help us SETTLE FOR A SUBSTITUTE. Paul warned us about ANOTHER GOSPEL, ANOTHER JESUS, ANOTHER SPIRIT and we do well to be AFRAID OF ANYTHING LESS THAN THE ORIGINAL TRUTH, GOSPEL AND HOLY GHOST. Today it is common to read the words, "AS GOOD AS" but there are many things that will never be replaced with some inferior items, materials or workmanship.

Jude told us to EARNESTLY CONTEND for THE FAITH once delivered to the saints. He was saying; there was, and is, only ONE ORIGINAL MESSAGE and we would do well to FIGHT FOR IT WITH ALL OUR MIGHT. Our day is one of shallowness, falsehood, shifty, sneaky speakers, make believe folks, and compromise. We are living in the midst of CARNALITY, DOCTRINES OF DEVILS AND DECEIT, and we must not accept some type of SUBSTITUTE, seeing our SOULS hang in the balance. I am calling each of us to more desperate prayer, searching the scriptures, commitment beyond anything we have known thus far. I am sounding the ALARM. It is time to AWAKE, PUT ON LIGHT AND TRUTH AS A GARMENT. We must be about HIS BUSINESS; ACCEPT NO SUBSTITUTES.

IF HE LOSE HIS SOUL, WHAT CAN HE GIVE FOR IT

Jesus was quite strong about the fact of losing our SOULS. That the world with all its wealth, precious jewels, elegant homes, nice clothes, bulging bank accounts, lots of applause and awards, could in no way ever EQUAL THE WORTH OF OUR SOULS. I have often wondered if any of us really grasp the MAGNITUDE of such a loss as the SOUL of mankind, especially seeing what a price HEAVEN HAS PAID TO RANSOM IT BACK. If all God wanted was some servants, HE SURELY PAID TOO HIGH A PRICE, for He could have created an entire race of angels to serve. There must be some MAJESTY involved with this SOUL THING, some WORTH beyond our ability to measure that would cause the GOD OF GLORY to become so involved.

I pray that each of us will somehow begin to realize how PRECIOUS THE PRIZE is; that TWO WORLDS are REACHING FOR THE SOUL OF MAN. Jesus seemed to believe that it would be possible for any person to LOSE THEIR SOUL just by living life and getting buried under THINGS. It seems His warning is full of care, as He wants us to see how easy it could happen. Nothing is stated about being VERY WICKED OR BAD, but just being human and getting caught up in the hustle and bustle of living. He seemed to think that the WORLD WAS NOT WORTH ONE SOUL and that if I would lose it, WHAT could I give in the EXCHANGE to get it back. The answer seems to be a cold fearful, NOTHING. Once I lose it there is nothing that can compare to its value, nothing that God would even think about accepting. This is why the PRECIOUS BLOOD OF JESUS should be sung about, prayed over and praised daily. I am PURCHASED by that BLOOD, COVERED by it, PURGED by it, IN COVENANT through it and NO DEVIL DARE VIOLATE IT. May God help each of us to take care of the condition of our souls!

IF YOU REALLY KNEW—YOU SURELY WOULD

Jesus began talking to the woman at the well and must have startled her with this statement; IF YOU KNEW WHO IT WAS TALKING TO YOU AND THE GIFT OF GOD, YOU WOULD HAVE...How many times has this type of thing occurred in our lives: IF I HAD ONLY KNOWN? So many times our own BLINDNESS or DEAFNESS to some situation left us doing the wrong thing, or doing nothing. How often we have felt so bad about something, when we found out the whole story, how many of us WOULD HAVE DONE DIFFERENTLY IF WE HAD ONLY KNOWN. There has been given to us so much information about the LORD, THE CHURCH, OUR MISSION AND HIS SOON COMING that none of us can really offer the lame excuse; IF I HAD ONLY KNOWN! God has called each of us to REPRESENT HIM to this dying world, to USE OUR RESOURCES for the advancement of HIS WORK FIRST, so that we cannot possibly claim IGNORANCE.

If the investor had known, he would have. If the pilot had known, he would have. If the householder had known when the thief would come, he would have. I could go on and on. The issue is clear to me; BECAUSE WE DON'T KNOW MANY THINGS, WE MUST BE ALERT, AWARE AND ABOUT THE WORK OF THE KING. The KING HIMSELF has told us to WATCH; FOR IN THE HOUR YOU THINK NOT, OR NOT WATCHING, HE WILL COME. I do not know what any day will bring my way, TRAGEDY OR VICTORY, but I have the opportunity to DO MY BEST FOR HIM IN EVERY SITUATION. In the book of the ECCLESIASTES we are told that anyone who watches the wind or studies the clouds, what they see can stop them from sowing and reaping. We must sow the seed and believe that God will cause it to grow. Don't let what we know or don't know stop us from doing His will.

FROM BONDAGE TO HIS BORDER AND BEYOND

The desire of our God has been shown to us through the nation of Israel: from the place of SLAVERY to SERVANTS OF GOD. The journey involves three places; Bondage, which we all have been involved with. Egypt is the BONDAGE PLACE, being slaves to some power or person or practice. God steps into our BONDAGE with a man and a message. MOSES for them, JESUS for us. God gave Moses a plan just like Jesus has given us a plan. A SLAIN LAMB, APPLIED BLOOD and FOLLOW THE CLOUD. All along the pathway God shows HIMSELF STRONG for the needs of the people, yet we must FOLLOW THE CLOUD. God gave the people their leader; he then spoke to them what he had heard from God. The people were blessed as they would comply with THEIR GOD GIVEN LEADERSHIP. I am quite sure that all here can tell that I AM NOT A MOSES but I am doing all I can to hear from God and follow HIS LEADING. I have read where God led them unto the BORDER of HIS SANCTUARY and no further. They had to make a choice; go, stay or return back to EGYPT. The same holds true for all of us now.

THROUGH THE CROSS we have been allowed to leave BONDAGE, and He has led us unto the BORDER OF HIS GREATER BLESSINGS. Now we must choose; go, stay or turn back to what we used to be. MAY GOD HELP US TO WALK ON INTO THE BEYOND. The BEYOND is that place where we walk by faith, in total trust and belief, knowing that the God who brought us out of BONDAGE and led us as far as the BORDER, now waits to see if we will FOLLOW THE LEADER into the BEYOND, INTO THE NEXT LEVEL OF LIFE. Considering how GOOD GOD HAS BEEN SO FAR, I am ready to move forward, for He has never failed us yet. Come on folks, the LAND OF PROMISED FULFILLMENT awaits us: FORWARD MARCH.

THE REAL NEED IS TO MAKE CONTACT WITH GOD

How often have we thrilled at the, story of the woman with the issue of blood, what was the key to her healing? I know the Lord told her "her FAITH HAD MADE HER WHOLE", but there seems to be more to it than FAITH. It seems to me that it was her faith that moved her into action, a faith so driven to TOUCH HIM, it caused her to overcome various obstacles to experience what she wanted from Him. I am sure many who were in that crowd that day had FAITH but it seemed to be divorced from ACTION. It seems to me we can possess a type of faith that does not help us because we refuse to put our so–called beliefs into action, using in real life situations OUR FAITH. In Mark 2, some men had brought a friend to get healed, but there was no access available unless they became somewhat desperate by going on the roof. After tearing the roof open, letting the cripple man down, these words shout at us, "Jesus seeing their faith."

So apparently our faith can be seen by the efforts we put forth to reach Jesus in some way. Faith really can only be real if it is willing to TAKE SOME RISK and SEEK TO GO BEYOND THE SAFE ZONES WE LIVE IN. He had no guarantee that Jesus would help him but their act of faith so moved the MASTER, he not only healed him but first FORGAVE HIS SINS. Jesus knew the first real need in his life was within, the cripple part was secondary, and it still is with JESUS. He did not come to fix the flesh although He often did it. He came to FIX THE SPIRITUAL FIRST. May each one of us use our faith to make CONTACT with Jesus, for from Him flows all we have need of. Take a risk and reach for Him, you will not be turned away.

TAKE HEED TO YOURSELF AND THE DOCTRINE

Apostle Paul warns us, as well as his son in the Gospel, Timothy, to be very careful about his personal spiritual life and to THE DOCTRINE. But WHY? To the early church the teaching of DOCTRINE was fundamental to the HEALTH of both the individual and the full body of believers. We must grasp that BIBLE DOCTRINES are a source of ongoing inspiration and constant adjustment to all believers. Our CREEDS AND DOCTRINES are absolutely necessary for spiritual growth as well as PROTECTION FROM PREDATORS WHO SEEK THE SOULS OF MANKIND. The Devil has been A DWELLER IN DARKNESS for a long time. He hates the LIGHT (DOCTRINE) and cannot work well with anyone who will WALK IN THE LIGHT. DOCTRINE ALLOWS SERVICE; for all true service must flow from BELIEF. We can really do nothing worthwhile unless we operate from our CONVICTIONS, which must come from our BELIEF SYSTEMS, WHICH IN TURN MUST COME FROM OUR CREEDS BORN FROM TRUE BIBLE DOCTRINE. Behavior comes from our beliefs, our beliefs must come from TRUTH, WHICH MUST BE OUR DOCTRINES. Our day has become one of EASY BELIEVISM, EASY DISCIPLESHIP AND SHALLOW BELIEFS. Our day is earmarked by CONSUMER ETHICS: THE CUSTOMER IS KING. Not so in this KINGDOM: JESUS IS ABSOLUTE KING AND HIS WORD IS THE RULE FOR CONDUCT AND BELIEF.

A man's life is the outcome of his thoughts, for the WORD STATES "AS A MAN THINKETH IN HIS HEART, SO IS HE." No wonder we are warned often about our THOUGHT LIFE AND WHAT WE ALLOW TO BE PUT BEFORE OUR EYES, ENTERING OUR EARS AND TOUCHING OUR HEARTS. Make sure you LOVE THIS DOCTRINE, FOR YOUR SOULS WELL BEING IS AT STAKE. TAKE HEED.

DARKNESS IS NOT A SIGN OF MISSING GOD

All of us want to walk in the Light of God and to please Him with all our hearts, but there are times when we seem to be forced to fellowship the DARKNESS. Some would tell us that we have sinned or have done something that missed HIS WILL, like the friends of Job did to him. We know from the end of his story that THEIR TALKS were not correct and even God told them so. To be forced to face the DARK TIMES in our lives should not cause us undo concern, for God has arranged for us to LEARN FROM EACH ASPECT OF LIFE.

It is always very confusing for me personally when I have tried to do my best, made the best decisions I could, tried to obey the Book and yet TROUBLE comes and the DARKNESS seems to be so DEEP. But there is a great verse located in Isaiah that shouts to all who may be dealing with the darkness now. It states "who among you that feareth the Lord, that obeyeth the voice of his servant, that walketh in darkness and hath no light? LET HIM TRUST IN THE NAME OF THE LORD AND STAY UPON HIS GOD." We are being told here that just because we fear and obey God, that will be no guarantee that we will not be forced to deal with THE DARKNESS. We can greatly honor or exalt our God in the DARKNESS by believing and behaving in such a way that the POWERS OF DARKNESS get no PRAISE FROM US AT THAT TIME. Our enemy always seeks for us to SAY SOMETHING OR DO SOMETHING during our testing times that will DISHONOR GOD, but we are told that we should TRUST GOD AND STAY UPON HIM. God knows where we are and what we are going through. He will not forsake us nor cast us away in those times of DARKNESS.

Keep walking your way through the darkness, for it has an appointed end as Job told us, "HE SETTETH AN END TO THE DARKNESS." PRAISE GOD FOR HIS MERCY!

MANY ARE CALLED BUT FEW ARE CHOSEN

It is always a grand thing when we are invited someplace, asked to be a part of some good event or even just to be asked to be a participant. We all enjoy the thing called INCLUDED: It makes us feel a little special. One of the best things to be INCLUDED in has to be the KINGDOM OF GOD. When Jesus came to this planet, He came with A MISSION, A MESSAGE AND A METHOD to accomplish HIS PURPOSES. I am so glad that through HIS CALL upon my life that I have been asked to BE A PART AND ALSO TO CONTRIBUTE to the fulfillment of HIS GRAND PLAN. To be called is not only an HONOR but carries with it an AWESOME RESPONSIBILITY. Most of us know that within ourselves we cannot accomplish whatever HE wants us to but THANK GOD, GRACE has been provided for our WEAKNESS. I know that God sees the end from the beginning and He knew all about each one of us: WARTS AND ALL. He knows what potentials lie in us as well as the tendency toward fear and failure. I want also to be CHOSEN and not just one He has CALLED, for God calls many but only chooses those FEW who are willing to DIE TO SELF. Because HIS WAYS are unlike ours, the battle rages daily.

We must deal with a world that tries to conform us into the WRONG IMAGE. Added to that, our own FLESH AND DESIRES OFTEN HINDER OUR PROGRESS. No wonder Paul called us to FIGHT THE GOOD FIGHT OF FAITH AND TO LAY HOLD UPON ETERNAL LIFE. MANY WOULD BE THE OPPOSERS to our winning that war. I surely want to make the RAPTURE and to be READY for the COMING OF THE LORD JESUS, so I must do whatever it takes to not INSULT THE CALLING with foolish living or wrong perceptions. I do not want to be a REPROACH to JESUS OR HIS WONDERFUL WORK: THE CHURCH. May God help each of us to really seek to be CHOSEN and not just CALLED. LET ALL EXAMINE THEMSELVES OFTEN.

IN THE LAST DAYS PERILOUS TIMES

The Apostle Paul wrote to his son in the Gospel about many things to watch for in the LAST DAYS. There seems to have been given Paul a POWERFUL PICTURE with regards to the conditions that would prevail in the days JUST BEFORE THE COMING OF THE LORD JESUS. A spirit of spiritual slumber would attack the world, a rising of RELIGIOUS TEACHERS, DENIAL OF THE APOSTOLIC DOCTRINE, SIN WOULD ABOUND AND NOT BE CHALLENGED BY PULPITS, MEN WOULD BECOME LOVERS OF THEMSELVES AND PLEASURES, MANY WOULD ARISE TO CHALLENGE THE VARIOUS PREACHERS OF THAT DAY, just like some did unto MOSES. Doctrines of devils would be spreading quickly and the TRUTH would be assaulted and insulted by LIBERAL FOLKS.

Perilous seems to be a correct word to show what we are facing today. TERRIFYING AND FEARFUL could also be added. When I read or listen to various DOCTRINES today being taught and CAUGHT by the people, I am SO THANKFUL, NOT ONLY FOR BEING TAUGHT THE TRUTH, BUT THAT God gave me a desire to WALK IN IT and to LOVE THE TRUTH. I know we are living in a pressure cooker but I also know; GREATER IS HE THAT IS IN US. The peril confronting all of us can be at times so subtle and sly, we can become buried beneath doing what is necessary and seemingly innocent. May God grant us to BE WISE, AWAKE AND CONCERNED about the WELFARE OF OUR NEVER DYING SOULS. Do not get sidetracked and waste your lives in doing something that could help you be lost; SPIRITUAL THINGS must be contended for. We need to realize that we are in the LAST DAYS, AND WHILE EVIL IS STRONG, GOD HAS PROMISED TO POUR OUT HIS SPIRIT GREATLY IN THESE DAYS ALSO. Seek God for a fresh anointing, eyes to see with, ears to hear with and do right.

A HOUSE DIVIDED AGAINST ITSELF CANNOT STAND

Jesus had just cast out a devil spirit from someone and the CRITICS jumped on it with great relish, stating that Jesus was in league with BEELZEBUB, THE PRINCE OF DEVILS. Jesus went on to explain the absurdity of their position; "WHY WOULD SATAN CAST OUT SATAN, WHY WOULD EVIL SPIRITS ATTACK EACH OTHER." His final point was this, A HOUSE DIVIDED AGAINST ITSELF WILL FALL AND BE A DISASTER. This truth holds for every area of our lives. Jesus spoke of how kingdoms, houses, and even people themselves must be in unity or they will experience failure of the worst kind.

A person who tries to share the affections, allegiances, or whatever with two or more purposes or persons will surely come to the parting of the road with one. If he or she is divided, they cannot give their best to either position, nor can they ever become personally what they might have with SINGLENESS OF HEART. God is TOO GREAT in HIMSELF to SHARE THE THRONE OF OUR HEARTS with any other personage, purpose or goal. As Elijah cried, "IF GOD BE GOD, THEN SERVE HIM, BUT MAKE UP YOUR MINDS, FOR A DIVIDED NATION, HOUSE OR PERSON, BECOMES EASY PREY FOR EVIL AND FAILURE."

The church is made up of various individuals with varying tastes, drives and agendas, but SHE must allow JESUS to be the CENTRAL UNIFYING FORCE for her life. The church must become one in PURPOSE, which should be the EVANGELIZING OF THE LOST, THE EDIFYING OF THE BODY AND THE MAGNIFYING OF HER LORD JESUS HIMSELF. God is not the AUTHOR OF CONFUSION but He can often become THE REVEALER OF ANY PRESENT CONFUSION when HE IS ALLOWED TO WORK AMONG HIS SAINTS. I am very concerned about the

PRESIDENTIAL RACE, as it has now REVEALED: the country is TOTALLY DIVIDED and in GREAT DANGER OF THE ENEMY BEING ALLOWED TO ADVANCE EVEN MORE. I ask you all to pray earnestly as we are now entering a DANGEROUS TIME OF DIVISION.

IN EVERYTHING GIVE THANKS: GOD WILLS IT

At different times, being thankful and the art of giving thanks seems to go against all that is within us; well almost all. The God within wants us to be thankful for HE KNOWS that a THANKFUL PERSON is not any easy prey for the PROWLING PREDATOR, THE DEVIL. Our foe seems to function best either in an atmosphere of DARKNESS or UNTHANKFULNESS. BOTH PROVIDE FERTILE SOIL FOR HIS WEEDS TO TAKE ROOT. Sometimes life seems to be working against the act of being thankful but God is worthy all the time and we should pause to consider ALL HE HAS DONE FOR US AND ALSO TO GRASP ALL HE HAS NOT DONE UNTO US.

All of us have our own lists that we could bring out that would show how we have been mistreated, didn't get a fair shake, seemed to get the short end of the stick here and there, but even with all these things, God HAS BEEN BETTER TO ALL OF US THAN WE COULD EVER DESERVE. Every day we live is just a gift from God. Whatever measure of health we now possess is surely better than we deserve; if we have any friends, food to eat, a home to live in, able to go to work, just to have a source of income, all these should move us to give thanks TO THE LORD.

What about our SALVATION, THE WONDERFUL GIFT OF THE HOLY GHOST, BAPTISM IN JESUS GREAT NAME, THE PROMISE OF HIS COMING, THE TRUTH OF LIVING FOREVER WITH HIM. Surely these things should provoke a PRAISE OF THANKS. God does not owe any one of us anything but a status of LOST FOREVER. But God is so good and merciful, He has reached down and made a way for any and all TO BE FORGIVEN AND FILLED with both JOY and HOPE. Our nation at the present is going through a TRAGEDY but we must grasp this one truth; WE ARE A SEPARATE KINGDOM living within another one and our rules and values are much higher and better. For this BE THANKFUL.

YE ARE THE LIGHT: OR ARE WE TOO LITE??

Today our society has become quite aware of the FAT in food, and the CALORIES, so that many products are now available with the labels crying; LOW FAT, FAT FREE, REDUCED CALORIE, OR LITE WHATEVER. Upon reading a recent U.S. NEWS AND WORLD REPORT about the question of the supposed SPIRITUAL REVIVAL in AMERICA, some of the statements caused much concern to this preacher. The article stated that the REVIVAL today seems to lack the fire and brimstone of years gone by and the RESULTS seem to be birthing a LOW CAL CHRISTIANITY unknown to the past or the pages of the HOLY WRIT. There seems to be a YEARNING FOR SPIRITUALITY but a very strong RESISTANCE towards COMMITMENT AND ANY TYPE OF REQUIREMENTS FOR DISCIPLESHIP.

America seems to be at ease with various forms of religious expressions that require LITTLE DEDICATION AND IMPOSE LITTLE OR NO GROUP IDENTITY. WOW! This writing has hit the nail on the head squarely; the days before the coming of the Lord Jesus will be earmarked by this kind of thinking. You're OK, I'm OK. God loves me the way I am and doesn't expect, nor demand, I CHANGE. To this LIE I SAY HOGWASH AND NOTHING COULD BE ANY FURTHER FROM THE TRUTH. Jesus asked the folks of His Day: "WHY DO YOU CALL ME LORD BUT YOU DO NOT DO THE THINGS I COMMAND OF YOU?" How can 'believers' ACCEPT JESUS on HIS CROSS AND REJECT HIM ON HIS THRONE as the LORD OF LORDS AND KING OF KINGS. His people must SUBMIT to HIS WILL, seek His WAYS and desire to PLEASE HIM WHATEVER THE COST.

Beware, lest we come up short, or the LIGHT we reveal is TOO LITE, HAVING NO REAL SUBSTANCE AND PUNCH. May God challenge all of us to RE–EXAMINE our lives. Have we taken out of the GOSPEL the areas that call for CROSS–BEARING, DEATH TO SELF, IDENTIFYING WITH THE SEPARATED ONES?

ONLY A SPOON, JUST A LITTLE SPOON

In the book of Numbers 7:14 it is told the story of what the tribes were to bring at the dedication of the ALTAR. TWELVE TIMES THE SPOON is mentioned as something to be included. The gift seemed so small and of little value yet, when anything is UNTO THE LORD, what may seem insignificant becomes WORTHY AND PRECIOUS. How often have we read in the WORD the various protests about I am nothing, or the least in my family, or what are they among so many (loaves, fish) and on and on the list goes. Yet it seems to me that the LITTLE SPOON had great value in the SERVICE OF THE LORD; AND SO DO WE. I know the feeling of being frustrated with my own LIMITATIONS AND RESOURCES, even to times when I felt so far behind various men and ministries and yet, God knows them and He still seeks to use me REGARDLESS.

ONLY A SPOON you say, yet that SPOON was needed. We are told to STIR UP OUR GIFTS, spoons can be very helpful here. The SPOON was to be PRESENTED TO THE LORD, to be at HIS DISPOSAL. SHALL WE DO LESS WITH OUR LIMITED LIVES AND GIFTINGS? The SPOON was to be GOLDEN; that means it must be real, valuable, reliable. In ourselves we seem to be worthless, but when dedicated to HIS WORK we become WORTHY AND VALUABLE, thanks to HIM. We receive IMPUTED RIGHTEOUSNESS AND IMPARTED HOLY GHOST POWER. HIS NAME IS PLACED ON US IN BAPTISM, OUR NAMES ARE WRITTEN IN HIS BOOK, ANGELS WATCH US AND HELP US Even though we are just SIMPLE SPOONS, yet we are called to be involved with the work.

ONE SPOON OF TEN SHEKELS OF GOLD, FULL OF INCENSE. JUST A SMALL SPOON BUT LOOK AT WHAT IT WAS FULL OF.

INCENSE: We are to be filled with the SPIRIT AND THUS OUR PRAYER LIFE, like incense, can be effectual and full. Incense indicates COMMUNION, A TRANSACTION of great value, and of PLEASURE TO GOD. May God help we LITTLE GOLDEN SPOONS TO DO OUR JOBS.

MERCHANDISE OR THE MIRACULOUS

In Isaiah 39:1–2, the king was visited by men from Babylon and Hezekiah gave them a guided tour of all his wealth and riches. It was a twofold blunder, for they were getting a grand picture of what could be had with an invasion. The worst part of the tour was simply and tragically this; RICHES were revealed but the MIRACLES were not even mentioned. The believer today must realize that the world we live in has GOLD, SILVER, RICHES, WEAPONS, SPICES, and TECHNOLOGY, but they really need and want what the CHURCH MUST HAVE ON DISPLAY—THE MIRACULOUS POWER AND PRESENCE OF GOD.

The world has much more of the natural things in life, but the SUPERNATURAL is missing. We must seek God to manifest HIMSELF in our midst more readily. We must also be willing to witness and talk about the many wonderful things that the SPIRIT HAS DONE. For visitors to come among us and only experience talent, gifted workers, songs wonderfully sung, music played well, sermons that inform and inspire only, is to fail to give them the one thing they DO NOT HAVE. Hezekiah felt that the visitors would be more impressed with his wealth than the various experiences he had from the LORD. TOO many people only see THIS WORLD, and need to feel, taste and experience the REAL SPIRIT WORLD. The story says, "HE SHOWED THEM ALL THAT WAS IN HIS HOUSE." He never shared nor showed ALL THAT WAS IN HIS HEART.

Babylon had gold but no PROPHET, merchandise but no MIRACLES, properties but no PRECIOUS ANOINTING OIL, many voices but not THE HOLY VOICE OF GOD. The cry of the world today has not changed from that of yesterday; "SIRS, WE WOULD SEE JESUS." Can we offer them ANYTHING LESS? May God have mercy on us for showing our MERCHANDISE AND NOT HIS MIRACLES…

TIS THE SEASON TO BE MORE THAN JOLLY

That time of year is once again upon us and it surely is a GRAND SEASON to say the least. To be JOLLY is surely in order, but that seems to me just the TIP OF THE STORY. While we can enjoy all the festivities that surround the CHRISTMAS SEASON, I think we need to be deeply reflective on WHAT IT IS REALLY ALL ABOUT. To think that the LIVING GOD came to earth to VISIT, VANQUISH THE DEVIL AND DELIVER THE CAPTIVES OF SIN SHOULD CAUSE US TO FALL DOWN ON OUR KNEES IN AWE AND WONDER. I am so grateful for this VISITATION FROM GLORY for it made possible the SALVATION OF OUR SOULS. God provided HIMSELF a BODY TO BLEED and DIE IN, thus providing a LEGAL WAY for HIS HOLY SPIRIT to descend and dwell within frail humanity. The entire story is so awesome, it borders on TOO GOOD TO BE TRUE, BUT IT IS TRUE.

Any of my readers who have had the grand experience of REPENTING, BAPTISM IN JESUS NAME AND BEING FILLED WITH THE PRECIOUS HOLY GHOST can testify to the truth of the matter. It really is JOY UNSPEAKABLE AND IT IS FULL OF GLORY — God in a human body called JESUS and then God in many bodies called the CHURCH. To think that God would come down into our world to SET US FREE AND THEN FORGIVE ALL OUR SINS AND THEN SEEK TO MOVE INTO OUR FRAIL FRAMES, SHOULD CAUSE US GREAT JOY.... Usually the PRICE PAID for any article will indicate the WORTH of the article. What must the VALUE be of our SOULS seeing the amazing price God has paid for them? The PRECIOUS BLOOD OF JESUS, THE Guiltless dying for the Guilty the Just for the Unjust, the Pure for the Impure, OH PRAISE GOD for this grand visitation and victory. During this season of holly, shopping, gift buying, card sending, trip taking, etc. PLEASE take some time and reread the Gospels and offer your own THANKS. This GIFT–GIVING began with GOD you know...

THE SPIRIT OF CHRISTMAS CAME FROM GOD ALONE

Well, the grand season will finalize very soon and I hope we all can grasp the real spirit of the season flowed down into our messed up world from the LIVING GOD OF GLORY. The real issue was and still is GIVING unto the UNDESERVING, UNHOLY AND THE NEEDY. I am so glad our GOD gave us HIMSELF wrapped in that little baby many years ago and now seeks to GIVE HIMSELF VIA THE HOLY GHOST, which is really, CHRIST IN YOU, THE HOPE OF GLORY. I know the MALL challenges the MAKER in an all out effort to direct us, but the SPIRIT of CHRISTMAS came from the MAKER, not from the MALL. The MALL may accommodate our efforts to purchase and give gifts, but it has a motive of PROFIT FOR ITSELF; OUR MAKER HAS A MOTIVE, THE PROFIT UNTO THE RECEIVER.

The INCARNATION has always been one of the greatest acts of God for it alone allowed the SIN DEBT of mankind to be paid for and canceled. What a GREAT GIVER GOD is and what PLEASURE He has received through His EXPENSIVE GESTURE. To think that God would step into a world that didn't really want Him or even understand the terrible need they had. Oh thank God for being so kind then and surely even today, we are really debtors to HIS GRACE AND GIVING NATURE. I pray that I won't be misunderstood in this article in regards to MAKER OR MALL, but I hear radio jingles and read paper ads all speaking about how to make this CHRISTMAS the best yet by PURCHASING THINGS or by GIVING YOURSELF the thing you deserve.

May God cause all of us to take some time and bend our hearts, heads and knees in offering THANKS UNTO THE ORIGINATOR of this grand season. MERRY CHRISTMAS TO YOU ALL.

THE PATH AHEAD IS FULL OF YESTERDAY

As the people of Israel, we too now stand upon a great place, the end and the beginning together. Like them, we too have yet to walk the untrodden path that lies ahead, but like them, we can now look back into yesterday and know that HE who hath called us OUT now calls us ONWARD. The God who has been so good to us, providing supplies, strength and the direction for our trek, will not leave us to face the future by ourselves.

I feel like Israel of the past, standing on the banks of the Jordan, thrilled with the past and somewhat wondering about the future. They spent 3 days on that bank recalling and consecrating themselves anew, and this should be now done by us. Let us examine ourselves, seeking to be very open and honest with the issues. They were told that God was about to do some WONDERS among them, so they had to get ready for them. THE WONDERS OF TOMORROW ARE TIED TO THE SANCTIFICATION OF TODAY. God is surely calling each of us unto a new surrender and dedication unto HIS WILL for our lives. We need to improve our praying, our giving, and be lifted to a new level of faith that will both honor GOD and defeat the DEVIL.

We must now recall; we are following the ONE who had a life full of PRAYER AND SERVICE. Can we seek to do any less and expect the same results? Our ABILITY, GIFTINGS, TALENTS AND POSITIONS will never be able to really replace TOTAL SUBMISSION and SURRENDER to HIS WILL. Israel did one more thing; they sent THE ARK AHEAD — not their fears or worries or skills. They followed the real LEADER, THE LORD HIMSELF. We are in a better place then they, we have GOD WITHIN our bodies. So as we go ahead HE does the same, so let us go forward in faith.

IF GOD BE FOR US, WHO CAN BE AGAINST US

I think it is time, maybe even past time, for the folks of the FAITH to take stock of what we believe, what has been promised to us and WHO IS REALLY FOR US. The ALMIGHTY GOD that spoke this world into being, the GREAT GOD who commanded the seasons, the weather patterns, the cycle of life for all creatures, HE IS FOR US. I think we all need to stop just attending church services and start being THE BLOOD WASHED, SPIRIT FILLED CHURCH that can become a threat to HELL and all its forces. I think we need a fresh vision of our job, what really is the purpose for us being who we are and just what has GOD allowed us to have access to.

I know our world is filled with vileness, wickedness, drug abusers — all sorts of sick stuff, IT IS PAST THE TIME FOR US TO GET FIGHTING ANGRY. We must seek God for a clearer understanding of OUR PURPOSE AND HIS POWER so we can at least try to accomplish the IMPOSSIBLE. Our city is overflowing with people who are held as slaves to sin and self, Jesus surely wants them to be freed. If the CHURCH doesn't arise, they will remain the PAWNS of HELL and we must surely just HANG OUR HEADS AND STOP SINGING OUR SONGS.

I feel like Elisha of old, crying out at the Jordan River, "WHERE IS THE GOD OF ELIJAH?" I am so hungry to attempt the ridiculous and radical, I want so much to believe that God will INTERVENE and show HIMSELF STRONG. Please PRAY for a new DRIVE WITHIN, A NEW HUNGER, A NEW LEVEL OF FAITH so that Jesus will be so honored in doing great things among us and the SLAVES OF SATAN will experience DIVINE DELIVERANCE. PRAY UNTIL SOMETHING HAPPENS IN YOU AND THEN ATTEMPT SOMETHING.

THE HIGH CALL OF GOD TO SINCERITY

David tells us in Psalm 51 that God desires TRUTH IN THE INWARD PARTS, THAT HIS PEOPLE BE REALLY SINCERE. The word SINCERE comes from an old English word: SIN(without) CERE(wax). In the olden days much furniture was hand made. If the wood was dimpled or flawed, the people would often blend WAX into the object and polish over it, it would be sold as first grade. The problem would only arise as the object was put near some fireplace or heat of some kind. God wants us to be clean–hearted, sincere in all our ways, so the HEAT OF LIFE OR TRIALS will not show a FLAWED VESSEL.

Today, many have a passion for SUCCESS, but not for being SINCERE, and God has a PASSIONATE INSISTENCE for it. Our world seeks to get us to be INSINCERE in business dealings, interaction with other believers and in numerous other ways. It seems like our SUNDAY WORSHIP faces MONDAY'S WARFARE, for public opinion is against all types of NON-CONFORMISTS.

SINCERE: Without deceit, no pretense, truthful, honest, genuine, real, to be in actual character as in outward appearance, no hypocrisy.

Insincerity robs all of us of true and real character forcing us to PRETEND, TO PLAY A ROLE — leaving us DISHONEST, SHIFTY, RESTLESS and poor ambassadors of CHRIST. We are also robbed of our INFLUENCE. GIFTS AND TALENTS, ETC. are nothing without the POWER OF INFLUENCE. We must PRACTICE HIS PRESENCE DAILY, and this will keep us SINCERE and the type of people that do HONOR THEIR GOD.

THOU DESIREST TRUTH IN THE INWARD PARTS. SO LET US GIVE GOD WHAT HE DESIRES...

IT IS TIME TO GIVE GOD WHAT HE REALLY WANTS

Today we often hear or read various slogans about what different organizations are looking for; the MARINES want a few good men, another branch says "BE ALL YOU CAN BE" and on and on it goes. The business world wants YOUR BEST, but GOD WANTS OUR ALL. I wonder, as we have entered into a new year, if we will GIVE GOD WHAT HE WANTS, or will we just offer the LEFTOVERS of our time, finances and abilities? Life seems to pressure all of us into some type of mold and seems to steal our best along with time. I feel each of us must make a fresh consecration in our hearts and heads to try to GIVE GOD WHAT HE WANTS. FOR ALL HE HAS GIVEN TO US shouldn't it be rather easy? We are such debtors to GRACE AND MERCY, we wouldn't even be alive but for HIS GOODNESS.

When Jesus came to the well in Samaria, He simply asked for some water, no great thing, but the lady was shocked over it. The RACE issue loomed too big for her at that moment, so Jesus had to get her involved with the bigger picture, HER PERSONAL SIN STATUS…I think so many times we offer some flimsy little excuses about why we can't GIVE HIM WHAT HE WANTS — that ANGELS MUST GO INTO SHOCK. Seeing that all the earth is HIS, all the wealth is HIS, ALL…ALL…ALL…ALL…EVERYTHING IS HIS ANYWAY. It seems amazing that the OWNER would ask us for one thing, seeing HE OWNS IT ANYWAY!

I think that God receives pleasure from our working with HIS SIMPLE REQUESTS and enjoys the fact that as we render unto HIM WHAT HE WANTS, He then is FREE TO FLOW INTO OUR LIVES WITH THOSE VERY THINGS WE SEEM TO NEED. We know our God is not STINGY,

BROKE, OR OUT OF POWER, but I think we hold the key to our receiving by the way we RESIST OR REFUSE when HE WANTS THINGS FROM US.

Let us give HIM HIS DUE, GIVE PRAISE, THANKS, WORSHIP, SERVICE, SACRIFICE, LOYALTY, LOVE FOR HIM AND OUR FELLOW MAN…

THEY SHALL MOUNT UP WITH WINGS

This often-used scripture has always challenged the believer, for most want to be able to live up above the earthly arena of life. The one key is written, THEY THAT WAIT, they that serve the Lord with life and lips, will surely learn the art of MOUNTING UP. I read an article about birds that stated, "THE HEARTS OF BIRDS ARE HEAVIER IN PROPORTION than the hearts of man or other animals." The reason given was, THE MORE THE BODY WORKS, THE GREATER THE DEMAND ON THE HEART WHICH CAUSES IT TO BECOME HEAVIER. Birds are very hard working creatures and so should the BELIEVER BE.

A LOFTY LIFE LIVED ON SPIRITUAL WINGS requires an ENLARGED HEART, WHICH MEANS CONSTANT FELLOWSHIP WITH GOD HIMSELF. If we are to live in the HEAVENLIES, TO ARISE we must ask God to give us a bigger heart. Our desires must be for SPIRITUAL THINGS and only A HEART that is after God will allow that.

In Psalms 119:32 the writer shouts, "I will run in the way of Thy commandments, when Thou shall ENLARGE MY HEART!" Unless our hearts get bigger, we will never be able to obey God in a perfect way, so we must seek God for a BIGGER HEART. In Ezekiel 36:25–26, we are told that we must have our hearts washed and cleansed first and then God will grant us a NEW HEART by taking out the STONY HEART. No person can ever FLY HIGH with a STONY HEART, we must have a NEW HEART and then God has promised to put within us A NEW SPIRIT.

God himself wants us to come up higher and learn HIS WAYS and that requires WINGS, which require a BIGGER HEART which calls for WASHING, REMOVAL AND RECEPTION of a NEW HEART AND SPIRIT.

VISION IS NECESSARY, BUT NOT ENOUGH

I often speak to this church about the value and power of VISION, but I feel I need to add — VISION BY ITSELF WILL NOT BE ENOUGH to bring to pass what has been seen, felt or heard. Jacob had that great experience at BETHEL, but when he had come out of his vision state, he then went to work by pouring oil upon that stone and promising God he would do various things. Jacob went his way for 20 years with no record of praying ABOUT THAT VISION. I cannot find that the VISION JUST CAME TO PASS by itself, there are things that we must do ourselves to see it happen. Faith without works is dead, being alone. I must seek to comply with HEAVEN in every way possible, I must put myself into the picture so the IMPOSSIBLE HAPPENS. I am not saying we can FORCE GOD, but I am stating, we can adjust our lives to be in ALIGNMENT with the VISION so DESTINY will be experienced.

When God spoke to Gideon about the victory he planned for him, Gideon still had to get involved and attack. We must surely hear from heaven, but then we must surely seek the WAY TO ACCOMPLISH VISION. INSPIRATION is not enough to live our lives by, although it is a must for us. I am very glad when a FRESH INSPIRATION hits me for from it, I can plan anew and get some type of ENERGY WORKING I didn't have before.

David had been told he would be the next king, but VOICE AND VISION by themselves would not be enough. Goliath would stand in the way, Saul would seek to slay him, many would try to hinder him, but God let David travel various roads until DESTINY would be tasted. We must have a VISION and allow it to INSPIRE US, to apply ourselves so we can see it come to pass.

WORKERS FOR THE VINEYARD NEEDED

The great story about the owner of the vineyard going out again and again seems to reveal the HEART OF GOD to us. The owner wanted workers; he went 3 or 4 times to get men into the field so that the harvest would not be lost. He had such a PASSION for the precious harvest not to be lost that he kept going out and hiring men to accomplish the job. God seemed to be ANXIOUS FOR WORKERS and he felt that each man could be doing something worthwhile if only given a chance to. He has a service for all to do and He wants all to come and be really involved with what HIS HEART DESIRES. One can see signs that say, "NO WORK" or "NONE NEED APPLY," but God doesn't ever say, "NO WORKERS NEEDED TODAY."

God wants us to realize that He will reward any service with blessings that can far exceed what we should receive. Those who came into the field at the 11th hour received wages that were more than they really deserved, but GOD IS ALWAYS BETTER TO THOSE WHO LET HIM MAKE THE DECISIONS. No one will ever get LESS than agreed upon, but many shall surely be blessed with much more than they have EARNED. We must consider — God's measures are not ours — they far EXCEED.

We must remember that God always sees OUR MOTIVE for doing HIS WORK, not just the fact that we complied. He looks into OUR HEARTS and sees WHY we do the work, it doesn't matter the length of time we have been working, ONLY THE MOTIVE MATTERS. AN HOUR WITH ALL OUR HEART IN THE WORK IS BETTER THAN A HEARTLESS JOB. May God help us to put our HEARTS into HIS WORK, for it is the only WORK that will last.

POSSESSION BY FORCE—INTENSE DESIRE

Jesus told us that since the days of John the Baptist, the Kingdom is actually gotten by force, and the VIOLENT TAKE IT BY FORCE. Some writers translate the verse to read; The Heavens have been suffering VIOLENT ASSAULT and the VIOLENT have been seizing it by FORCE. We might be somewhat perplexed by this verse for we are often told that the things of God must be achieved by FAITH, NOT FORCE. But what is real faith?

FAITH IS A LIVING POWER FROM THE HEAVENS THAT GRASPS THE PROMISES GOD HAS GIVEN.

This verse seems to be promoting the power of DEEP INTENSE EARNESTNESS. It seems to be saying God has provided whatever we might need, BUT THEY MUST BE CONTENDED FOR AND GRASPED BY THE DESPERATE. Remember, the Devil hates God, and HIS KIDS, so he will not just stand by idle while we walk through his turf and pick up various weapons that will defeat his work. He will seek to deter all of us one way or another. Usually, after a few defeats or attempts, a thought will come to us like; YOU MISUNDERSTOOD, YOU'RE NOT WORTHY, GOD DOES NOT DO THAT ANYMORE, DON'T BE SO RADICAL. Remember, our adversary has one powerful weapon; HIS VOICE, and he uses it over and over again — many times through well-meaning folks in the CHURCH.

We cannot secure various spiritual helps without FAITH, but it is also true that FAITH and VIOLENCE are inseparably CONNECTED. REAL FAITH must become a FORCE that can deal with any and all obstacles, mainly LACK OF INTENSITY...

NO preaching has done much good that doesn't cause the hearers to PRESS FORWARD AND TAKE WHAT HAS BEEN OFFERED, BY FORCE. We must become INTENSELY EARNEST or settle down into HOPING SOMEDAY that something better will occur. Let's PRESS ON, GET DESPERATE FOR THE PROMISES TO BECOME A REALITY IN OUR LIVES, NOW…

WITH ALL YOUR GETTING — GET UNDERSTANDING

I have often preached from this passage regarding UNDERSTANDING, yet it seems to expand with more study. We all seek to acquire many things; education, character, homes, cars, clothes, spirituality, etc., but the most valuable and impacting must be TO GET REAL UNDERSTANDING. There are so many things in life that seem to baffle our brains, steal our time and impact us for the worse, we really need UNDERSTANDING.

When we look at life itself, we need it; facing the future with all of the real scary uncertainties, we need it; trying to find what is best for us, we need it. Considering we have AN UNDYING SOUL, we must have UNDERSTANDING to know how to use our time wisely. We must face the truth about the upcoming JUDGMENT OF CHRIST — the fact that we will be giving JESUS an answer for what we have done as well as all we failed to do. It wouldn't be so scary if JESUS had not personally given us the POWER to do all we need to do and the great MESSAGE OF ACTS 2:38. God is going to require an answer from all of us — how we USED OR MISUSED OR ABUSED the finances we had and the TIME we received as a gift from GOD.

I pray that all of us will seek God for REAL UNDERSTANDING, for it alone has the power to change and correct various issues in our lives, ASK PAUL! Once the LIGHT comes on in our brains and hearts, we can alter actions and accomplish more for HIS GLORY. I am so glad that God is so very patient with me, I am glad He allows me to learn from my mistakes so I can do better. GET UNDERSTANDING FROM GOD.

WINNING AND LOSING CAN BE VERY EASY

I was reading today about the nameless prophet who came down to the altar that Jeroboam had erected in Bethel to keep people from going up to Jerusalem to worship, fearing they would leave him because of feelings being kindled from the REAL PLACE. He had set up a CALF to be worshiped, but he forgot what had occurred before with Moses on the mountain and Aaron making the calf for the people. If we do not learn from history we are usually forced to REPEAT HISTORY and that can be very costly and fatal.

Out of the crowd came the nameless prophet and he then spoke against the altar. The king became very furious and tried to grab him, but God made his hand to wither. He pleaded for mercy and the prophet prayed for him and he was healed. The king asked him home, but God had told him not to go. Leaving the scene, we find him resting under an oak tree, sometimes like we do after we have had a victory; we rest awhile, take off our armour and let down our guard. A person must keep alert especially after a victory, for our enemy will not let up even though he has just lost a battle. HE WILL BE BACK with a new plan.

The battle with SELF, SIN AND SATAN must be REFOUGHT OFTEN, so beware of taking it easy after a FRESH VICTORY. An OLD PROPHET came to him, lied in the NAME OF THE LORD; the young prophet went home with him, God spoke and told him he had DISOBEYED and then HE WAS SLAIN BY A LION. He had won a great victory for God and then lost in the next battle. It can and does happen often to all of us. BEWARE OF RESTING UNDER THE OAK TREE OF PAST VICTORY, KEEP YOUR ARMOUR ON AND BE ALERT. Do not trust in your Gifts, talents or genius, but rather in walking in TOTAL OBEDIENCE, for that path is SAFEST…

TROUBLE CAN BE SUCH A FRIEND

I am sure that most of those reading the title will think I have lost it for sure, but I feel I have found it. While we seem to waste so much energy trying to avoid problems, troubles and things we deem unpleasant, the truth is TROUBLE HAS BUILT WITHIN IT A BLESSING FOR ALL WHO WILL DEAL WITH IT HONESTLY. Trouble can surely reveal ourselves quite painfully and quickly, to say the least. Trouble has a way of making us reach BEYOND our small imposed limitations and really accomplishing so much more.

DIFFICULTY is not a dirty word, for we are MADE STRONG BY WHAT WE ARE FORCED TO FACE, not by what we have managed to sidestep and avoid. Trouble has within itself a CHALLENGE we all need to propel us into a higher level and to tap into our LATENT POTENTIAL lying dormant. We all have a built-in desire to just coast, to do what has to be done and take life easy. This has never been the WAY OF GOD. He has always managed to put HIS PEOPLE into some tough situations, yet He always brings them out—and much better I might add.

Various TRIALS and TESTS are never sent to us so we can CRASH and FAIL, but rather to EDUCATE us about the WEAK AREAS of our lives and to REVEAL the POWER OF GOD that is available for the asking. So often, God forces us to come to the end of ourselves so we can be cast upon HIM; this way HE IS GLORIFIED, SATAN IS DEFEATED and WE ARE HUMBLED and made PURER AND WISER. Often, as I have read the various stories of the BIBLE, I have been impacted to a better view and understanding of life. I am so glad for JOB, DAVID, DANIEL, MOSES AND ABRAHAM. I have received so much again and again from the recorded events of their lives, through it all GOD HAD BEEN WORKING. I therefore will accept trouble from HIS HAND.

SPEAK THE TRUTH IN LOVE, THE WHOLE TRUTH

Truth seems today a very scarce item in all types of situations. From our childhood, we have been taught that we should always be truthful. Truth has a grand power to LIBERATE the bound, to free the guilty and TO HONOR GOD. We have witnessed so much scandal of late coming down from the WHITE HOUSE to the CHURCH HOUSE that so many folks don't seem to believe anybody no matter what their office or position might be. We who name the wonderful name of JESUS should do our very best to be FILLED WITH TRUTH so that we may ever be HONORABLE and GODLY.

I know we live in the midst of corruption on many levels, but the CHURCH must be untainted by the little and big LIARS that fill our land. We have been granted a fabulous treasure called the TRUTH and we will surely give an accounting on how we used or abused it someday.

In the world of religion, so many have never come into contact with the WHOLE TRUTH as we have. The great message of One God, Baptism in JESUS NAME, the infilling of the HOLY GHOST, SPEAKING IN TONGUES, the GIFTS OF THE SPIRIT; no wonder that the writer of JUDE tells all of us that we should seriously, violently and earnestly CONTEND FOR THE FAITH. He knew that in our day, men would arise to challenge any APOSTOLIC TEACHING AND EXPERIENCES and would pervert the GOSPEL. The greatest blessing JESUS ever handed down to us has to be the TRUTH; about life, ourselves, HIMSELF, eternity, judgment, catching away of the beautiful church, the final defeat of the devil, evil and sin. We should be THANKFUL for the TRUTH, not be afraid of standing up for it and living our lives according to its STANDARD...

BE PREPARED

Some of you may recognize the title to this article from your younger days with the BOY SCOUTS, for that was their motto. The Lord often told his followers to be ready, be prepared and be watching. In our everyday lives, this little motto really should be applied to all our situations. I personally hate to be caught off guard in any number of situations, especially when it has to do with SOULS AND THE KINGDOM…

The story of the ten virgins shows us how terrible it will be for any and all who FAIL TO BE PREPARED FOR THE COMING OF THE BRIDEGROOM. I know all kinds of symbols have been given to the story, but our LORD seemed to be saying, "BE PREPARED," but for WHAT? All were virgins, all took vessels, all had oil and all were waiting for the bridegroom. So what is the lesson? I think JESUS was telling us be TO BE PREPARED FOR DELAYS—for us to be equipped with enough oil to last us if, per chance, A DELAY OCCURRED. The WISE, we are told, had TAKEN EXTRA FLASKS OF OIL with them. They planned for the POSSIBLE DELAY, the FOOLISH did not and this made all the difference in the story.

Another point of value is this; IN OUR GREAT HOURS, WE CANNOT BORROW WHAT WE NEED, WE MUST POSSESS IT FOR OURSELVES. In times of trial and testing, we cannot BE SHINING WITH BORROWED OIL AND LIGHT. Another person can not give us their faith, their power or their oil, for they need all they have for themselves. WE ARE CALLED TO BE WATCHFUL, for when we least expect it, A DEMAND can be put on us and then we must have enough of this–or–that to accomplish the task. "BE YE READY" often fell from JESUS' LIPS, and I do not think HE ever played with words, HE MEANT WHAT HE SAID, therefore, let us take heed. We must be able to deal with DELAYS, check the oil you have, if you're low, get some more…

JUST HOW SMART ARE THE SUPPOSED SMART FOLKS

Before you jump up and kill me for the above title, please hear me out. I am not against learning, training or advancing into various fields. What I am asking is similar to what JESUS asked in HIS DAY: HOW IS IT YOU CAN DISCERN THE SKY AND THE UPCOMING WEATHER, BUT YOU CANNOT DISCERN THE TIMES YOU ARE A PART OF? It seems to me that this generation, with its intense pursuit for knowledge, has somehow missed the FOREST FOR THE TREES. It seems that we are thrilled about learning the various secrets of OUTER SPACE and staying very ignorant about INNER SPACE. What does it really matter if we grasp secrets about everything or anything that has to do with TIME and miss what we need to know and experience regarding ETERNAL THINGS...

The JEWS studied the COMING OF MESSIAH and yet when HE CAME, they missed HIM totally. They LOVED AND STUDIED THE LAW yet when the LAWGIVER ARRIVED, they attacked and crucified HIM. We spend millions on WHERE WE CAME FROM and don't seem to give a flip about WHERE WE ARE GOING and HOW WE PLAN ON GETTING THERE. Our world buries itself into areas of investigation and does not seem to care about SPIRITUAL MATTERS. Yet WE ARE THE OFFSPRING OF DEITY AND THEREFORE WE, TOO, ARE SPIRITUAL BEINGS.

We all have a DESTINY that reaches far beyond today, things and stuff yet the EVIL ONE seems to be FOOLING FOLKS with a QUEST that is just a SHAM. Jesus said; what does it profit to gain the WHOLE WORLD and then LOSE OUR SOULS—or WHAT can we give in EXCHANGE FOR OUR SOULS? He felt our SOULS were so precious that HE WAS

WILLING TO SUFFER AND DIE to SET US FREE and allow us to be INFILLED WITH HIS HOLY SPIRIT.

SOMETIMES, THE BEST EXPERTS CAN BE VERY IGNORANT about the most important things.

THE ISSUE IS NOT OUR SIN—IT IS THE TRUTH

Jesus told folks in HIS DAY that THE TRUTH had the power to set people free, nothing else can do it. God does not seem to have much problem with our failures and sins, for He has provided THE BLOOD AT CALVARY to cleanse from every sin, but the GREAT PROBLEM seems to be in getting the human race to face the TRUTH about our SINS AND SELVES. While THE BLOOD awaits to cleanse, it is kept waiting for us TO ADMIT, CONFESS AND QUIT the practices that are UGLY TO GOD. It is not enough for us to be correct about DOCTRINE, for the RELIGIOUS OF JESUS DAY were that, but THEY refused to be TRUTHFUL about themselves. Jesus told them they were of their father THE DEVIL and would act accordingly, but WHY? THE DEVIL we are told is a LIAR and there is NO TRUTH in him, which really means, THE DEVIL IS LYING TO HIMSELF, REFUSING TO ADMIT THE TRUTH ABOUT HIMSELF, SO HE LIVES HIS OWN LIE.

SIN is really a LIE, for we refuse to do what God has said, in fact, many feel that God doesn't REALLY MEAN WHAT HE SAYS, SO HE CAN BE REPLACED WITH ONE'S OWN OPINION. We lie to ourselves when we DENY that we are in trouble, sinning our lives away and saying, "I'M not so bad, not as bad as such and such." If we refuse to admit our terrible condition before GOD, we cut ourselves off from the MERCY that GOD OFFERS SO FREELY. We then become SELF-DECEIVED and God is HINDERED in helping us, for without CONFESSION and a real DESIRE to change, we cannot experience the GREAT GRACE that awaits us.

The DEVIL, nor OTHERS, nor THE CHURCH, nor THE WORLD are the real problems, OUR UNWILLINGNESS to ADMIT and QUIT our LYING ABOUT OURSELVES in many areas of our lives IS. Remember, HE THAT COVERS HIS SIN WILL NOT PROSPER, BUT HE THAT CONFESSETH AND FORSAKETH, SHALL FIND MERCY...HONESTY STILL PAYS WELL.

NOT FOR SALE AT ANY PRICE

I was reading once again the grand story regarding the WICKED AHAB, THE NASTY JEZEBEL AND THE SUFFERING SAINT NABOTH. It seems that the people of GOD are often called upon to live by precepts that the WORLD will look down upon and usually do whatever it can to make us look like FOOLS and hopefully MAKE US FALTER. Hell loves to laugh at any who take God at HIS WORD and try to live by it; challenging our understanding and our compliance to it seems to be the order of the day.

Israel had been instructed never to sell their land, for it did not belong to them anyway. The LAND WAS THE PROPERTY OF THE LORD — simply a gift from HIM for their use. It was a SPECIAL INHERITANCE and it became very special as generations came and went. IT WAS NOT FOR SALE, NEVER, AT NO TIME, NOR FOR WHATEVER THE PRICE OFFERED. Hell has not changed the HATE it carries if any are unwilling to part with whatever GOD HAS PROVIDED. Even though the places and people have changed, the battle still rages; HELL WANTS ANYTHING WE HAVE THAT GOD HAS GIFTED US WITH. For NABOTH, it was a vineyard next to the land of AHAB, but king or not, God had told him through the past — NOT FOR SALE. The king returned home, sucking his thumb and went to bed like the BABY he really was — A KING IN NAME, BUT A SLAVE IN ACTIONS. His wife then wrote letters, had NABOTH lied on, then taken out and stoned like STEPHEN. Like all dishonest bums, AHAB thought he had won, but GOD IS NEVER MOCKED. Up the path came ELIJAH to denounce the deed and tell of future retribution.

WHAT HAS GOD BLESSED YOU WITH that you should not, cannot, put up for sale? The APOSTLE'S DOCTRINE, HOLINESS, SEPARATION, JESUS NAME BAPTISM, HOLY GHOST WITH TONGUES, REAL REPENTANCE AND PRAYING OFTEN — these are TREASURES handed down to us. We must not SELL OUR INHERITANCE to this world. NEVER!

THE GOSPEL ACCORDING TO ME

I know that there is but ONE GOSPEL, it is the gospel that PETER, PAUL and the rest of the APOSTLES preached, and there have not been any AUTHORIZED REVISIONS since. The NEW BIRTH, which includes both water and spirit, the DEATH, BURIAL AND THE RESURRECTION of JESUS, REPENTANCE OF SIN, HOLY LIVING, CRUCIFYING OF OUR FLESH all follow in the WAKE OF THE GOSPEL.

The GOOD NEWS for men is that God has been willing to PAY OUR DEBT ON THE CROSS, THEN OFFER US THE OPPORTUNITY TO REPENT, WASH AWAY SINS IN BAPTISM AND THEN FILL EACH OF US WITH HIS HOLY SPIRIT. That is THE GOSPEL ACCORDING TO GOD AND HIS WORD. The problem lies with the church, for the WORLD usually doesn't attend church, nor read the BIBLE, but they do read our lives—VERY CAREFULLY AND DAILY. So the issue must be clear. What is the GOSPEL that is being preached, lived and shown, ACCORDING TO ME? Can a lost world look at our actions, attitudes and attire and GET THE RIGHT MESSAGE FROM US? I know many of us can point to various verses to defend our doctrinal positions, but I would like to go beyond that—am I living THE WORD, am I DISPLAYING DOCTRINE with the way I conduct my business, can my word and promises be trusted? For THE LOST must be shown truth in our lives first if they are going to believe THE BIBLE.

We must be LIVING EPISTLES, seen and read of men. We cannot live TWO LIVES, DRESS TWO WAYS, LEST WE BECOME PRETENDERS of the worst kind—BEING DECEIVED AND THEN BY DECEIVING OURSELVES. Paul wrote that we are to be manifestly declared to be the EPISTLE OF CHRIST, can we answer this in honesty and conviction? May God help all of us not to add to the confusion of the LOST WORLD by PREACHING A FALSE GOSPEL.

A BLESSED CRAVING— HUNGERING FOR GOD

All of us have known the power of really CRAVING something; usually it is some type of dessert or food that we could do without. Cravings can also be SPIRITUAL and these are the most beneficial, for the things of ETERNAL WORTH should have our attention and hungering now. Paul wrote this wonderful truth roaring from his deepest being, OH THAT I MIGHT KNOW HIM. Having met Jesus on that road, being talked to directly, then to be called into ministry and being so greatly used by GOD would have satisfied many of us I'm sure. But for Paul, DYING DAILY, and yet CHRIST LIVED IN HIM, created a yearning and desire that moved him until his dying day. I wonder if that HOLY CRAVING is alive in us today? I wonder if we are just kind of COASTING until the rapture, glad to be saved, but not really hungry for HOLY THINGS.

I think we all need to pray for a new DEEP YEARNING OF THE SOUL so that we may become whatever HIS PURPOSE for us may be. Most of us would agree; nothing of any real consequence can happen without some type of DESPERATE DESIRE, whether in SPORTS, BUSINESS OR CHURCH. I often wonder if our lack of yearning is because we may fear the PRICE attached to such CRAVINGS. We must ask ourselves: HOW WELL DO I KNOW JESUS, or HOW WELL DO I REALLY WANT TO KNOW HIM? Remember, knowing about JESUS is not the same as KNOWING HIM, for to be involved with JESUS will affect our lives totally. Our speech, actions, attire, attitudes, responses, will all come into view from that interaction with JESUS. Being we have received such MERCY and much LONG SUFFERING, WE SHOULD BE QUICK TO GIVE THE SAME. The more we KNOW HIM, the better we will be at NOT BEING CRITICAL, HATEFUL, OR HARMFUL. Our DESIRES REVEAL OUR VALUES...

HEY, WHAT IS IN THIS SITUATION FOR ME?

I am sure all of us have at one time or another either felt like the above title or have heard from someone else that was the way they were thinking. It seems too easy to become somewhat SELF–SERVING in so many areas, especially when it comes to CHURCH. Our society has taken the attitude that people are SUCKERS for doing things for others and not getting paid for it, or at least thanked. God spoke to Israel in Mal 1:10 about their unwillingness to even open the temple doors for nothing, or to kindle a fire upon the altar for nothing. He concludes with this remark, "I HAVE NO PLEASURE IN YOU, NEITHER WILL I ACCEPT AN OFFERING AT YOUR HAND."

God does not think the way our world does, He feels we should not have to get paid to serve, nor be given a bunch of thanks for doing our duty. They seemed to become so selfish and benefit oriented, they just wouldn't do very much without COMPENSATION. They had been so blessed and enriched, they had lost a sense of DEVOTION and DEDICATION. When people lack something better and bigger than themselves, they seem to lose INTEGRITY, HONOR and ETHICS, to say very little about SACRIFICE and THANKSGIVING.

We are always blessed and better anytime we go beyond what is REQUIRED, FOR GOD LOVES A CHEERFUL GIVER; that applies to more than money. How long has it been since some of you gave something to this church besides a check, how about doing something that would interrupt your little SCHEDULE? Have you called the sick, how about visiting some, came and worked on the grounds? If we are too busy to do a few extra things, we ARE TOO BUSY with things that don't matter anyway. INNER JOY comes from doing what you don't have to and doing it without COMPENSATION...

REALITY IS WHAT IS NEEDED, NOT THEORY

There is no doubt in my mind that JESUS gave the world THE GREATEST STANDARD of LIVING that has ever been seen. Jesus had no advantages as the world counts them. He was born into poverty and lived under the LASH of Rome. He knew very well what it was to live without. Yet He so impacted the world as to cause various people from all walks of life to leave their places of vocation and security, to follow HIM into an invisible kingdom with a lifestyle so diverse from all around them. He displayed such a LOVE for people, seeing the WORTH IN EACH, THOUGH IT SEEMED HIDDEN from the naked eye. He was the PERFECT SERVANT and as such, became the SUFFERING SERVANT in order to accomplish THE PURPOSE OF GOD.

I wonder if we have missed the trail in that we have not been willing to give ourselves to HIS CAUSE, possibly because we have failed to grasp it. Willingness to be LAST, giving away our power and human wisdom does not appeal to any of us for sure. A RIGHT ATTITUDE is a must if we are to impact and lead others in the WAYS OF GOD. A WRONG ATTITUDE IS really PLACING VALUE ON THE WRONG THINGS, mainly things that have to do with time and matter. Remember, in GOD'S KINGDOM, the VALUE of things will always be judged by THE CROSS PRINCIPLE so no flesh can GLORY and all must be willing to DIE TO SELF DAILY.

The PATH Jesus has called us to walk is not easy for our flesh, but if we through the SPIRIT mortify it, walking that path will conform us into the IMAGE OF JESUS and allow HIS WILL to be done in and through us. The PROBLEM is we all seem to pursue UNWORTHY MOTIVATIONS that vie for our time, talent and money. May we give this world A LIVING REALITY, PURPOSE WRAPPED IN FLESH, and not talk that accomplishes nothing but VANITY…

ARE YOU WILLINGLY IGNORANT?

The Apostle Peter writes to us about certain folks who, knowing previous events that brought the Judgment of God upon their generation, seem to willingly choose to REMAIN IGNORANT. It is one thing to be IGNORANT about any area or situation in life due to lack of training, learning or whatever, but when the facts are clearly SHOWN AND KNOWN, it then puts us into an area of "WITHOUT EXCUSE." To overlook or ignore certain facts regarding God and what He demands is to PLAY THE FOOL with our ETERNAL WELFARE. Peter talked about folks who ASKED DUMB QUESTIONS, WALK IN THEIR OWN LUSTS, SCOFFERS LAUGHING ABOUT THE COMING AGAIN OF JESUS and others who knew the HISTORY of the past and just chose TO BE WILLINGLY IGNORANT.

We must ask ourselves, WHY WOULD ANYONE CHOOSE TO BE IGNORANT about things VITAL and NEEDFUL TO THEIR SOUL'S WELL-BEING? The answer must be that these folks do not believe the WORD, FEEL NO OBLIGATION TO COMPLY, OR HAVE AN IDEA THAT MERCY AND LONG-SUFFERING do not really exist. These folks seem to think that THE LOVE OF GOD will FIGHT AND BEAT DOWN HIS HOLINESS—which is totally crazy, for NO ATTRIBUTE OF GOD FIGHTS OR VIOLATES ANY OTHER. God does not clash within HIMSELF; it is dangerous to be WILLINGLY IGNORANT.

To interpret various scriptures to make them blend with bad behavior or loose lifestyles will bring a bad ending to a foolish life. Many today, even in this church, are twisting verses into CURSES so the WORD now is SUBJECT to their reasoning and they can go on living UNCRUCIFIED LIVES, which of themselves INSULT THE SACRIFICE that was made for us at CALVARY. I lift my voice in CONCERN AND WARNING: any who choose to be WILLFULLY IGNORANT cannot ever make APPEAL TO THE GOD OF THE BIBLE…

THE GREAT HOAX — A CROSSLESS CHRISTIANITY

Most folks know that Jesus died on the cross to set man free from sin, but so many today are totally ignorant of the DIVINE DEMAND for the CRUCIFIED LIFE of all believers. Jesus did die in our place, but not so we could go merrily living our lives in pursuit of UNCRUCIFIED FLESH; that has been the GREAT LIE. So many churches do not ever call their folks to any type of DENIAL and usually speak quite unkindly towards those of us who seek to bring our desires into alignment with the BIBLE. Jesus told all who would become HIS FOLLOWERS TO DENY THEMSELVES, TAKE UP THEIR CROSS AND FOLLOW HIM.

We are seeing the growth of a generation that knows nothing of SELF–DENIAL and even talks degradingly about it. Many seek to DIVORCE being a CHRISTIAN from all types of suffering or problems; this is totally incorrect. We would all do ourselves a big favor by not trying to DEBATE DEITY. For God, who spoke from the FLESH OF JESUS, told us that our DENIAL of SELF would be a price of being HIS DISCIPLES. So many today who promise LIBERTY are themselves SERVANTS OF ALL TYPES OF CORRUPTION; be careful who you are listening to. We do not need to try and REPACKAGE THE GOSPEL so it can be less offensive to a world that seeks to GRATIFY ITSELF DAILY. DENIAL is not a bad or dirty word.

The BABY BOOMERS who know very little about God, who want church to be ENTERTAINING, NEVER COSTLY OR AT THE WORST, CHALLENGING, CANNOT tell God or His people what they want and how they want it—it just won't fly folks! The CROSS has power to TRANSFORM all people and we must seek to conform our lives to be PLEASING TO GOD, for nothing else really matters but that. May God help us to teach and live the whole truth.

THE SPIRIT MOVED HIM: NOTHING MOVED HIM?

The first part of the title has to do with SAMSON, for the Spirit of God would come upon him and grant him SUPERNATURAL POWER to accomplish various feats that would help his people. It seems to me that we all would be the kind of people God would have us to be if we would allow HIS SPIRIT to move on us FREELY. I am totally convinced that many of us either resist the SPIRIT or we are so caught up with life, we have become too INSENSITIVE to be MOVED UPON. Remember, HIS SPIRIT CAME DOWN ON JESUS LIKE A DOVE, not a HAWK. We must become a type of landing platform for the POWER TO SETTLE UPON. This surely requires an upward looking attitude, a type of outlook that constantly desires THE THINGS OF HIS SPIRIT; for without HIM, WE CAN DO NOTHING. Let us seek to be worthy and wanting of the OTHER WORLD TO SETTLE UPON US, that we may be able to become vessels or conduits through which HIS POWER CAN MOVE ON AND INTO.

The second part of this title has to do with the life of PAUL; he had been told that all types of troubles awaited him as he went ahead to ROME. It was the desire of the church for Paul not to go, but his response was, NONE OF THESE THINGS MOVE ME; even in the face of possible death he was determined to do THE WILL OF GOD. This type of attitude is also necessary in each of us if we are to accomplish something for God. I must be MOVED UPON and yet, in other areas, I MUST NOT BE MOVED—what a great combination. Our adversary often seeks to move us off our Promised Land, from great truths and from sacrificial living; usually showing us some other folks who don't live like we do. He is a LIAR, A DECEIVER, A BACKSLIDER of the worst kind, we must SUBMIT TO GOD—RESIST HIM AND HE WILL FLEE, SO ASK FOR THE POWER TO MOVE UPON YOU AND FOR STABILITY TO STAY UNMOVED.

SATAN IS AFTER WHAT GOD IS USING

I know that our enemy seems to be on our trail so often, but we must remember; he can't have everything he desires, he's not an ALL–POWERFUL FOE. We all know the grand story of Jesus raising LAZARUS from the dead, but have you read the rest of the story? Many JESUS HATERS were also plotting to kill LAZARUS, too, because HE WAS A LIVING TESTIMONY to the GREATNESS OF JESUS — he just had to be eliminated. Many times our foe seeks to FRUSTRATE US, STEAL OUR JOY or HURT OUR WITNESS through mistakes we make; he has got to GET RID OF US SOMEHOW. All through the WORD, when God would bless any person, SATAN WOULD NOTICE and go to work, for a BLESSED person usually is a PRAISING PERSON, and that will never do, for HELL HATES any GOOD PRESS GOD MIGHT GET FROM US.

Satan sought to get rid of JOB because he refused to practice EVIL, he resisted suggestions to do wrong, and that honored GOD and laid Satan in the dust. He was hated by Satan and became the OBJECT OF HIS OBJECTIONS, SLANDER AND HATE. Sometimes we do not realize why we are battered so much, why crazy things come our way or even why we seem to be TEMPTED so harshly. You must realize, more is at stake than just the TRYING OF YOUR FAITH. EVIL seeks to bring a REPROACH TO GOD, SHAME TO HIS CHURCH AND GUILT TO US.

When Joseph was tempted by a MARRIED WOMAN he fled, lost his coat, but kept his INTEGRITY. That moment became a grand MONUMENT that became a PLATFORM for the future. Be careful, when you get careless with your character, more is at stake than the MOMENT. TWO WORLDS ARE WATCHING YOU.

RENEW A RIGHT SPIRIT WITHIN ME

Most of us know that David prayed this request in Psalm 51 after his tragic episode, but I think we all need to do this type of praying for ourselves. I feel such a great need within myself to be refreshed, revived and rebaptized with FRESH FIRE AND ZEAL. I know that God has no desire for HIS WORK to suffer at the hands of COLD AMBASSADORS who are just going through the motions but not really doing their job. We have been given a mandate from our MAKER to make HIM known to every person we meet, and we must do THE BUSINESS OF OUR KING with power and passion. We are dealing with ETERNAL issues, but we do not have ETERNITY to get the work finished; we must become very INTENSE AND EARNEST about LOST SOULS.

I am feeling a WEIGHT settling upon me and I have been seeking God for a FRESH TOUCH of HOLY GHOST POWER to be the kind of witness Jesus deserves. The price He paid for TOTAL REDEMPTION on the cross was too great for we believers to be slothful with our calling. God intends for us to be MIGHTY, and knowing the powers of evil that would resist us, He surely desires that we FIGHT them with HOLY ENABLING. In your praying, please pray for a FRESH HUNGER and THIRST, for an ANOINTING that will accomplish HIS WORK THROUGH THE SPIRIT and not in our flesh or ideas.

God will surely empower us just as He did in the book of ACTS if we will sincerely seek for it. I know I want to be more for Him and I will be, for He has promised power and ability to any and all who will pay whatever the price is to obtain it. Please join with me in PLEADING AND BELIEVING AND PURSUING our LORD until He breaks forth among us in DEMONSTRATIONS OF DELIVERANCE for mankind.

THE GREAT KEY—HUNGERING FOR GOD ALONE

I feel that we are in a great battle for our church and also for the great harvest of souls God has promised to us. We must now apply ourselves to three things: SUBMIT to God; RESIST the devil and INSIST on seeing and experiencing THE FULL IMPACT of a FRESH VISITATION from God as we sincerely desire to BECOME A HOLY NATION unto HIM. "Pursue" is the word used in regards to HOLINESS, it will not come to us, we must honestly and hungrily SEEK HIS HOLY WAYS for our lives.

I know that God wants to bless, but before that He desires his people to be DESPERATE FOR DEITY. We must begin to take INVENTORY within every area of our lives to insure that we are not harboring DESIRES, DRIVES OR PRACTICES that could be ABHORRENT TO OUR GREAT GOD. Before we begin to see God moving into the SOUL-SAVING WORK, we must be honest with Him about getting our own lives in line with HIS WAYS. Please seek God for yourselves, asking for a PURGING and CLEANSING of everything and all things that might be a HINDRANCE to HOLINESS. We must have a visitation from above to be able to accomplish HIS PURPOSE for our day. It really lies within our own laps…ask JESUS to take A WALK THROUGH THE GARDEN OF YOUR SOUL. He is in love with us—nothing coming to us from HIS HAND will ever be EVIL, FOR ALL THAT HE SEEKS TO DO WITHIN US WILL ONLY HELP US TO BE MORE LIKE HE WANTS.

Getting closer to GOD is what we need and should want, for why would any person who has been spared and saved want to JUST GET BY? I want to know HIM and be FILLED WITH THE FULLNESS OF GOD, but this will cause us to make MAJOR ADJUSTMENTS—to say the least. In view of what is possible to people who HUNGER AND THIRST for GOD, how could any of us be SATISFIED just with CHURCH SERVICES? ASK, SEEK, KNOCK, for ANSWERS have been promised.

THE NEED OF THIS HOUR— DESPERATION

To be desperate means to be driven by a great desire or need, to become DRASTIC in actions over a given situation. It can also mean to become extremely dangerous such as a violent criminal, etc., yet all of the above should now be applied to the church living in this present wicked hour. What could happen if we who say SALVATION AND DELIVERANCE has been entrusted to our hands, begin to act upon our CALLING AND MISSION?

We can see the terrible condition that our generation is in, groping without hoping for something better than material toys and little prizes in life. We as the CHURCH must now become DESPERATE to be a LIFE–CHANGING FORCE within our city and thus honor the great sacrifice JESUS MADE FOR ALL MANKIND. We must view our position as one of GRAVE AND SEVERE RESPONSIBILITY for we ALONE possess the ANSWER to the problem of SIN and death. The Gospel is the POWER OF GOD in this world and it is greater than all the forces of evil, but if we who hold onto it refuse to DELIVER AND DEMONSTRATE it to this lost world what will be our FATE? What would be done to that person who had the serum that could now heal all types of CANCER and yet never told anyone? We who have been brought out of DARKNESS and DEATH must SHAKE OURSELVES and become FILLED WITH HOLY DESPERATION to do whatever we can. Remember, God has not told us to do anything He would not equip us to accomplish, we must believe GOD WILL BACK UP HIS WORD.

The FOUR LEPERS, WHO sat in front of the city, took a leap into DESPERATION without any promise of mercy or provision. We have been given GREAT, EXCEEDING PROMISES so that we should go forth BOLDLY. Please pray for A DEEP SENSE OF DESPERATION to get a hold of all of us, for unless we become DESPERATE the world will be lost, God dishonored and His desire frustrated: This must not happen!

THE DEVASTATING WEAPON OF SATAN—DISTRACTION

I have been hearing a lot these days—on the radio as I drive—regarding the use of our cell phones. The constant message is the same; DO NOT BECOME DISTRACTED WHILE YOU ARE DRIVING AND USING YOUR CELL PHONE. All sorts of advice is given; utilize the hands free option, don't dial, use recall, etc. It seems many accidents have been occurring because of BEING DISTRACTED. It seems to be a very old problem. How often I was told as a child, "WATCH WHERE YOU ARE GOING, PAY ATTENTION TO WHAT YOU ARE DOING, PLEASE STOP TURNING AROUND." All children seem to get DISTRACTED very easily, but I think we adults need to be told more often, "PAY ATTENTION TO WHERE YOU ARE GOING, WHAT YOU ARE DOING, HOW WE ARE DEALING WITH PURPOSE AND MISSION."

Our enemy seems very subtle in his approach to us and we can get SIDETRACKED OR DISTRACTED while doing a good thing or a right thing. It is very possible for us to try in some area of life, but become DISTRACTED from what is MORE IMPORTANT AND VALUABLE. We must ever be on guard about GOOD OR BEST, ETERNAL OR TEMPORAL, NEEDFUL OR ABSOLUTE. We can get way off course just by being DISTRACTED, OR AS BRO. TENNY HAS OFTEN SAID, "WE MUST KEEP THE MAIN THING THE MAIN THING."

There's no sense in our being great in minor things, yet off-key in MAJOR THINGS. If our enemy can get us off the primary and into the secondary, we can FAIL BADLY. How many times have we heard people excuse themselves for not doing the job assigned? "I just got DISTRACTED..." a terrible thing when a doctor is cutting on you and he gets a phone call and leaves. I know GOLFERS who get hot if they are in any way DISTRACTED by movement, noise or whatever. FOCUS is something we all must work at, for the enemy tried to get JESUS DISTRACTED with petty things, hurtful people and such, but HE SET HIS FACE STEADFASTLY TOWARD THE CROSS. We can do anything; let's focus afresh!

JESUS: THE UNCHANGING MIRACLE WORKER

The Bible surely testifies of Jesus from Nazareth as the GREAT MIRACLE WORKER. And from HIS BIRTH, HIS WALK, HIS DEATH, HIS RESURRECTION AND ASCENSION, HE remains the same in POWER, GLORY AND PURPOSE. We must somehow re-examine HIS LIFE, MISSION and what we have been called to accomplish. I am often stunned by the UNBELIEF found in the church regarding the area of MIRACLES TODAY. For some reason I think we have been sold a terrible bill of goods by both the devil and mankind; those who have traded FAITH FOR INTELLECT and THE SUPERNATURAL FOR REASON.

CONSIDER: The birth of Jesus was miraculous. His life was filled with miracles, His death and resurrection were both miracles, His going back into the heavens in a cloud was surely a miracle. Perhaps, the most STAGGERING OUTSTANDING MIRACLE has got to be the arrival of the HOLY GHOST at PENTECOST. To think of how these men, who had run away a few weeks prior, now could stand in the public eye and PROCLAIM JESUS LIVING WITHIN THEM and wanting to LIVE IN OTHERS has got to be A GREAT MIRACLE. The NEW BIRTH that was both PROMISED AND REQUIRED FOR ENTRANCE INTO THE KINGDOM, HAS MIRACLE WRITTEN ALL OVER IT.

CHRISTIANITY IS NOT A RELIGION UNLESS THE FOLKS WHO SAY THEY ARE CHRISTIANS TRADE THE MIRACULOUS FOR REASON, INTELLECT, AND THE TRADITIONS OF MEN WHO DO NOT HAVE THE SPIRIT.

CHRISTIANITY IS THE LIFE OF GOD WITHIN A PERSON, THE UNVEILING OF THE HEART AND WILL AND NATURE OF GOD

HIMSELF. FIRST WITHIN THE BODY AND LIFE OF JESUS, THEN WITHIN HIS FOLLOWERS. Anything less than this is not REAL CHRISTIANITY, it is simply RELIGION which is a belief without THE MIRACULOUS. If we forfeit the SUPERNATURAL WE ONLY HAVE RELIGION; POWERLESS AND PATHETIC.

JESUS: THE UNCHANGING MIRACLE WORKER, PART 2

Our world desperately needs the SUPERNATURAL OF GOD and not the counterfeit of Satan. When Jesus began his work, it was with miracles, and the CHURCH also began its work with miracles. I am convinced that somewhere along the way, our enemy introduced some type of concept that became an accepted practice: that the MIRACLES, SIGNS AND WONDERS OF JESUS AND HIS CHURCH HAD SOME TYPE OF ENDING. I must stand against this LIE! Jesus has not in any way changed. His message is the same. The church has the same AUTHORITY AND POWER given to it by JESUS — so what is the problem?

We have been fooled into thinking that the mind and intellect can run the church, that what it really needs is BUSINESS MEN, GIFTED SPEAKERS AND SINGERS AND PLAYERS, DEDICATED FOLKS TO MAN THE VARIOUS STATIONS; BUT WE HAVE MISSED THE MOST IMPORTANT PART — JESUS.

The church is His, the message is His, the method should still be the one He used for Himself and the early church, which to me should be MIRACLES, SIGNS AND WONDERS. The Bible is a record of miracles and of DIVINE INTERVENTIONS IN BEHALF OF HIS PEOPLE. The story of ISRAEL'S DELIVERANCE WAS A SERIES OF MIRACLES — the Red Sea, forty years of manna, water from a rock, Jordan rolling back, Jericho falling apart and on and on.... Only when they tended to lean on their flesh did the miracles stop, but upon repentance God would again WORK HIS WONDERS. We must begin to SEEK GOD FOR HIS POWER TO WORK IN OUR MIDST and ask for our faith to be purified so that our level of expectation can be increased until HIS GLORY COMES UPON US and the lost will be drawn to HIM. Every Revival since Pentecost has been one of MIRACLES AND SIGNS.

THE LESS IS ALWAYS BLESSED OF THE GREATER

The above statement comes from the days of ABRAHAM and speaking regarding being blessed by the PRIEST OF THE LORD. I feel today, as I REFLECT back over TWENTY YEARS being the pastor, that I HAVE BEEN BLESSED BY you and not the REVERSE. When we came here, you had been through numerous men who had PASTORED and LEFT; you had been through quite a lot. Then came into your midst this loud, excited and expectant guy who had never PASTORED anywhere but was convinced 'THIS WAS THE WILL OF GOD FOR HIS LIFE.' You have been so kind to us, you have prayed for us and loved us, put up with my ways and antics. Even when you could have become upset you stayed with us, GOD BLESS ALL OF YOU. I know We are CELEBRATING MY 20 YEARS, but to my way of thinking, the CELEBRATION should be for ALL YOU FAITHFUL FOLKS who have stayed and prayed. I am the LESS, you are the GREATER, SO I HAVE BEEN THE RECIPIENT of so many blessings and not you. I wish to give a great big THANKS to everyone who has been with me for these years. MAY GOD BLESS YOU.

I took a trip down MEMORY LANE today and pictured the old building that first greeted us, then the various folks that have since passed on or moved away. I saw in my mind so many who found mercy here, then for some reason FELL AWAY. May God still talk to all of them and call them back to HIMSELF. I attended the MANY FUNERALS I had to speak at, and some very sad feelings swept over me, but DYING IS A PART OF LIVING. I thought of all the folks I have BAPTIZED and CHILDREN that I have had the pleasure of DEDICATING. 'WOW, HAS GOD BEEN RICH TO SOMEONE AS LITTLE AS ME!' PLAYS, PARTIES, MUSICALS, REVIVALS, SEMINARS, PRAYER MEETINGS, SONGFESTS, MISSIONARIES, PREACHERS, FOLKS NEEDING A HAND OR HANDOUT; my plate has not only been full, but God has allowed MY CUP TO RUN OVER. THANKS AGAIN, for being so good and kind to us. I AM A BLESSED MAN.

THE POWER OF A FRESH VISIT WITH ANOTHER

As most of you know, I have been gone preaching to a number of SMALL, HOME MISSIONS CHURCHES and I have been so IMPACTED by the visit there. I have a greater appreciation for all these wonderful people who stick with the message, the place they are called to and the amazing SPIRIT OF SACRIFICE that was so apparent in each place I preached. I felt that God had put it upon my heart to go and try to help any way I could. But I feel that I AM THE REALLY BLESSED ONE, for it has allowed me to SEE YOU MORE CLEARLY and see the GREAT BLESSINGS that our GOD has surely poured out upon this assembly. Let me give all of this church family a GREAT BIG THANK YOU for being YOU, for staying with me and the APOSTOLIC MESSAGE. Thank you for your FAITHFULNESS in GIVING; I guess I did not grasp how much this church gives to the work WORLDWIDE.

Many of the people I met told me how often they visit our WEB SITE, how often they read and use MY ARTICLES in the bulletin, how many TAPES they order from this church and HOW BLESSED they have been because of the TEACHING AND PREACHING that has RESOUNDED from this pulpit. I realize that YOU ARE THE ONES TO BE THANKED, for you have listened and learned and changed for the better. We who PASTOR can get very BLINDED to just how WONDERFUL OUR CHURCHES really are, because we see so many things undone or not really right—LIKE MISSING THE FOREST FOR THE TREES. I have been asking God for FORGIVENESS FOR NOT BEING MORE THANKFUL AND APPRECIATIVE for this church and all you have done for the work in other places and here, too.

YOU ARE GREAT FOLKS, NOT PERFECT, BUT WANTING TO IMPROVE—and for that, I SALUTE YOU IN THE LORD. Thanks for sharing me with other places, for loving my wife and I and for supporting me and giving so much. I LOVE YOU MORE THAN YOU KNOW.

ARE YOU SAVED?
MAKING ANY REAL PROGRESS?

While the title of this little article may seem to pose 2 different questions, they are really part of each other. To be SAVED is to have experienced the SUPERNATURAL TOUCH OF GOD, responding with TRUE REPENTANCE and WATER BAPTISM IN JESUS NAME, FOLLOWED BY THE GREAT INFILLING OF THE HOLY GHOST. With such a wonderful event occurring within anyone's life, PROGRESS would seem to be an automatic thing, but that is not the case. Many who have really been BORN–AGAIN have, for many reasons, not made much PROGRESS in their walk with the KING, mainly because they have not become aware that PROGRESS was part of the package. We would think it quite strange if a couple were blessed with a new baby and then 4 years later, it still made baby sounds, still crawled and still did all the normal things that newborn babies do. In the natural realm we expect growth and progress, and if that is not happening, we begin to search for the reasons why. I feel it is long overdue that many of us begin to ask ourselves some tough heart–searching questions:

- Am I any more CHRIST–LIKE now then I was when I first was SAVED?

- Have I put away some things from my life that I used to do knowing that I should be more consecrated than when I first began?

- Do I really LOVE JESUS with more intensity and desire than at the first?

- Have I become more aware of my personal responsibilities to the CHURCH, THE KINGDOM and THE LOST OF THIS WORLD?

- Has my PRAYER LIFE improved in quality and quantity, or is it still unenjoyable?

- Has my GIVING increased, has the SPIRIT OF SACRIFICE found a FRIEND within me?

- DO I DELIGHT in SERVING JESUS or is HE just an ESCAPE FROM ETERNAL DAMNATION?

- Am I an ASSET TO THIS CHURCH, do I really LOVE CHURCH, does my ATTENDANCE reveal my attitude about MY REAL PRIORITIES?

WHAT IS THE REAL ISSUE? "THE REAL TRUTH?"

Today, we are being challenged and charged by the peddlers of PROSTITUTE CHRISTIANITY that the teaching of the APOSTOLIC CHURCH, to which our LORD JESUS committed HIS TEACHINGS to, did not fully grasp them and, therefore, were really totally wrong. I have heard and read much about the attack upon PETER, THE EARLY CHURCH AND EVEN APOSTLE PAUL, HOW WRONG THEY ALL WERE and how today the MESSAGE must be much more PALATABLE and LESS OFFENSIVE.

The people we are now to be TARGETING do not want CONFRONTATIONAL CHURCH AND TO BE CHALLENGED with some type of BIBLE TEACHING that DEMANDS THAT REPENTANCE AND BROKENNESS MUST ACCOMPANY EVERY MOVING TOWARDS GOD. This is now being FROWNED UPON and even LAUGHED at by these so-called PROPHETS OF PROSPERITY AND CHURCH GROWTH, BUT I stand up against all these FOUL SPECIMENS of DECEIT.

"TAKE HEED TO YOURSELVES AND THE DOCTRINE," was what PAUL shouted to TIMOTHY, FOR IN DOING SO YOU SHALL SAVE BOTH YOURSELVES AND THEM THAT HEAR YOU. Hearing goes far beyond listening to words, it really means DOING WHAT YOU HAVE BEEN INFORMED ABOUT. "WHY CALL ME LORD AND DO NOT WHAT I COMMAND YOU?" was what JESUS asked. I think HE is still asking that of this generation. We need to REVISIT our BASIC BELIEFS about what it takes to be REBORN and what kind of lifestyle we should embrace THAT WOULD HONOR HIM, WHO HAS BEEN SO KIND TO BRING US INTO HIS GREAT FAMILY.

This essential issue of CORRECT DOCTRINE is not some hollow cry from some old FANATIC PASTOR, but the TREMBLING SHOUT from one who sees on the HORIZON the COMING OF THE LORD JESUS for HIS BRIDE, WHO HAS MADE HERSELF READY. We need to become VERY SERIOUS about allowing any type of teaching to take us away from the book of ACTS and THE CLARION CALL TO HOLY LIVING. I could care less about all the folks who have now walked away from TRUTH, MODESTY AND HOLINESS, I cannot alter the truth, I must comply or die eternally.

REMEMBER THE KING'S WORDS

I realize this title could apply to a multitude of situations, but I am thinking of one in particular—the killing of the boy, ABSALOM. David had been mistreated terribly by him even to the point of being chased from HIS THRONE and being ATTACKED in an effort to KILL HIM. If anyone had a seemingly right to REVENGE AND PAYBACK it would surely have been DAVID. In this story, David gives a command TO SPARE THE BOY ABSALOM for THE SAKE OF HIS FATHER DAVID—WHO I MIGHT ADD WAS THE KING.

I think we have a picture of the LOVING HEART of our GREAT GOD who, although so many have mistreated and been ugly to, yet HE desires that none perish, that they be treated as KINDLY as possible, FOR HIS SAKE. David so loved his wayward son he could not just kill him, so he tells the troops to DEAL GENTLY FOR MY SAKE WITH THE YOUNG MAN. A soldier finds ABSALOM hanging by his hair in the bow of a tree and REFUSES to strike him down, REMEMBERING THE KING'S WORDS. Joab gets mad, goes and kills the boy and brings so much sorrow to the HEART OF DAVID—and a GREAT RIFT comes between the two. God seems to be showing us; MERCY REJOICES AGAINST JUDGMENT and God would have US to show mercy and patience to many who have HURT US.

REVENGE belongs to God and sometimes when we are harmed and taken advantage of, we all can find ourselves wanting to PAY BACK and get the situation fixed. It is not an easy thing to let things go, but A SOFT ANSWER TURNETH AWAY WRATH and Jesus gave us a real picture of how we should receive injustice. THE KING has charged us also with many things we SHOULD and SHOULD NOT do, the pressure is on all of us: Shall we keep the KING'S word or do what we feel needs to be done? May God help us to PLEASE GOD in each and every situation, especially when PROVOKED.

THE TRIUMPH OF THE WICKED IS SHORT

The wicked and evil seem so many times to get by, even to the place of prosperity and smugness. The word tells a different story though for GOD IS JUST AND HOLY, so nothing is missed by HIM. There are so many times in life when trying to be HOLY and live in tune with RIGHTEOUSNESS SEEMS TO MOCK EACH OF US. We must view these seeming injustices with the TRUTH: WHATEVER IS SOWN SHALL SURELY BE REAPED — not one person will ever get by. The terrible situation that our nation is being forced to deal with is not the end of the story; GOD WILL HAVE THE LAST WORD. I have often been challenged and even provoked by the ability of wicked-working folks who don't seem to be in the hot water and troubles that so many GOD-SERVING SOULS seem to be. I must not allow seemingly senseless episodes in life to overwhelm me and steal my dedication to the LORD AND HIS WAYS.

The truth has been recorded, THO' THE WICKED PROSPER, IT SHALL BE WELL WITH THE RIGHTEOUS. INJUSTICE does not have the power to INVALIDATE the great precepts that in time will PREVAIL. All through history God has shown over and over again — RIGHTEOUSNESS EXALTS A NATION and SIN IS A REPROACH TO ANY PEOPLE. Folks who want to practice EVIL sow the seeds for their own DESTRUCTION, for the LAW OF SOWING AND REAPING works regardless of anyone. REMEMBER, JESUS told us HIS KINGDOM was not of this world and neither could it, or would it, function in the same way. MIGHT DOES NOT MAKE RIGHT, the WAY UP IS DOWN, THE HUMBLE HAVE HIS ATTENTION, THOSE WHO LIVE BY THE SWORD DIE BY THE SWORD, THE SERVANT SPIRIT is the spirit that JESUS demonstrated and DEMANDS of his children.

I thank God for HIS KEEPING-POWER, HIS GREAT MERCY AND WILLINGNESS to work within each of us until we, too, can be LIKE HIM. DELAY is NOT DENIAL, GOD WILL HAVE HIS WAY EVEN NOW.

PROVERBS 26:2
THE CURSE SHALL NOT
CAUSELESS COME

The present time of trouble and sorrow should not cause any of us to challenge the GOODNESS OF GOD, but rather to examine our own hearts and lives. The verse above tells us that NO CURSE OR TRAGEDY is allowed to arrive just by itself, but rather it is THE OUTCOME OF SOME ACTION, REASON OR RIGHTEOUS ACT OF GOD. In LAMENTATIONS, 3:33 it says that God does not AFFLICT WILLINGLY IN ORDER TO CRUSH OR DESTROY mankind, but rather to call us to SEARCH OUR WAYS AND TURN AGAIN TO THE LORD.

Many times we seem to get angry or upset at what seems to be senseless situations, but we must bring into our reasoning THE ALL MIGHTY GOD WHO IS FULL OF WISDOM AND LOVE. Did not JOB shout to us down through the ages, "SHALL WE RECEIVE GOOD FROM GOD AND NOT EVIL?" At times of hurt, sorrow and loss, we seem to forget the fact that we have received so much UNDESERVED GOOD, and then when some EVIL ARRIVES we get upset. For some crazy reason when we feel GOOD, BLESSINGS, PROGRESS and SECURITY should just come our way, we feel it should be this way, but GOD IS LORD OF GOOD AND BAD. WHY some innocent folks should be made to suffer and be made to deal with wickedness has been the challenge of the ages. I feel the BELIEVER ALONE has the proper perspective on the issues — THE LORD REIGNETH, LET THE EARTH REJOICE.

I do not have any answers as to WHY this nation has suffered the RECENT ATTACK and WHY so many have been killed or crippled. All I know is the WORD says, "NOTHING COMES TO US CAUSELESS" and GOD has seen something that needed to be dealt with. He is also the LORD OF LIFE. Life itself flows from HIM ALONE, He has the right to do or allow anything that seems PROPER FROM HIS HIGH AND HOLY PERSPECTIVE. My heart has been moved with sorrow and wondering, but I REFUSE to CALL GOD INTO QUESTION, for that is the work of a FOOL. GOD IS TOO GOOD TO BE UNKIND, TOO HOLY TO BE VILE AND TOO POWERFUL TO BE DEFEATED. I must bow my head and say, "LET ME — LET US — SEARCH OUR WAYS AND LET US RETURN TO THE LORD, AMEN."

THE LORD SHALL BE THE HELP OF HIS PEOPLE

Surely as the events of recent days continue to unfold in tragedy and loss, we are all being forced to face the very stunning fact, THERE IS NO REAL SECURITY FROM ATTACK. Our nation is still reeling from the terrorist activities and the horrible aftermath, but to the people of GOD, NOTHING HAS CHANGED REGARDING OUR SECURITY AND FUTURE.

God has often allowed various measures to be taken that could and did cause people to look in another direction, UPWARD. Trouble has the ability to shock and terrify to the point we humans realize we cannot get along without HIS HELP. I heard the other evening that BIBLE sales had increased 300 % and the answer was, PEOPLE ARE NOW LOOKING FOR COMFORT AND STRENGTH. What a great time for the CHURCH to step up and SHOUT, "GOD IS A VERY PRESENT HELP IN THE TIME OF TROUBLE." God has allowed the stage to be set for HIS TEMPLES TO TESTIFY to all. The USA has been attacked, but NOTHING CAN SHAKE OR DESTROY THE CHURCH.

I have been praying for us that the LORD would visit us with a FRESH THIRST for an OLD- FASHIONED VISITATION of the HOLY GHOST and a HUNGER FOR HOLINESS FROM ABOVE. I, for one, desire to be CHANGED and become a LIVING CHANNEL for the POWER to flow into and out of. We must seek GOD to visit us with CONVICTION, CLEANSING AND FILLING so HE WILL BE GLORIFIED and we will be EDIFIED. We must arise to the occasion, cast off the GARMENTS OF SLEEPINESS AND WORLDLINESS and seek to be CLOTHED AFRESH with BROKENESS AND HUMILITY. Please be in prayer not only for our NATION, but also for the CHURCH — it is time for US TO ARISE.

IN TIMES LIKE THESE, WE NEED A SAVIOUR

The present situation regarding the killing of so many folks, the impending search and possible war with the TERRORISTS, has positioned this land on the brink of a possible disaster. I know for sure, the GREAT GOD OF GLORY has set the stage for mankind and also the completion of all that has been planned for the last days. I am not smart enough to declare with positive accuracy the recent events with regard to PROPHETIC IMPORT, but I am sure this has been A GIANT WAKE UP CALL for we AMERICANS.

I am moved by pictures and news that have come my way, yet I am very deeply moved by the TOTAL ABSENCE of NATIONAL REPENTANCE and the fresh SEEKING OF GOD. We see signs everywhere; "GOD BLESS AMERICA," but to me the underlying story does not include BY ANY MEANS, BROKENNESS AND WEEPING OVER OUR WAYWARD WAYS AND OPEN SINS. I have yet to hear any PREACHER call this nation BACK TO GOD IN CONTRITION and IN THE SEARCHING OF OUR WAYS. God is TOO HOLY AND WISE to allow us to be BLESSED so we may now continue in things that are DISPLEASING and SHAMEFUL TO HIM.

Surely, we must search out our own ways, our deceitful hearts, and plead with our KING to SHOW US WHERE WE HAVE NOW ERRED and grant us GRACE AND COURAGE to make any alterations before HIS HOLY THRONE. I have asked God to help me, and also our church family, to become GOD HUNGRY and HOLINESS HUNGRY so that from the ashes of pain and woe, we can break into a dimension of POWER AND REVIVAL. It is time for us first to THANK GOD THAT WE DO HAVE A SAVIOUR and that HE IS THE ONLY ASSET WORTH COUNTING UPON, FOR HE WILL NEVER LEAVE US NOR FORSAKE US. May there come into our hearts a GREAT PRAISE and may it come out of our LIPS AND LIVES, JESUS IS LORD.

FAR IS NOT DISTANCE, BUT RATHER A DIFFERENCE

I have spoken on this wonderful truth to this church family about 2 or 3 years ago, but I feel I need to revisit it once again. To so many of THE PEOPLE OF GOD, HE can seem at times so far removed from us, or that HE is not interested or even listening. This type of thinking did not have origin with HIM, but rather from HUMAN BRAINS or worse; HATCHED FROM HELL'S LIAR. Paul told the folks at ATHENS, we could all feel after HIM, though HE BE NOT FAR FROM ANY ONE OF US. Far does not have to do with GEOGRAPHY OR DISTANCE since God fills all time and space. DISTANCE CANNOT be the issue, but rather DIFFERENCE.

When in any area of our lives, whether in ATTITUDE OR ACTION, we FEEL THAT SENSE OF DISTANCE; God has not moved away; we have become so different from HIM we begin to think HE HAS MOVED. Judas was at the last supper, but WHAT A DISTANCE existed between him and JESUS! His heart was so UNLIKE JESUS a great gulf developed and drove him to his terrible deed of BETRAYAL. You can put an APE and an ANGEL into the same room, but although close in space, A GREAT DISTANCE would exist. Why, you might ask? The answer is simple…THEY ARE SO UNLIKE EACH OTHER the DIFFERENCE CREATES DISTANCE even though both are very close to each other.

Often in our lives we can be in the same room or even at the same table with folks and yet we sense a DISTANCE there: we are so different—unlike each other in tastes, likes and various areas, we actually become very uncomfortable. The same thing happens in a CHURCH SERVICE when sinners are exposed to HIS PRESENCE. The great difference between them and JESUS causes them to want to leave or be somewhat uneasy. I know in my own life, when I am out of joint in some area or practice, I FEEL SO FAR AWAY FROM GOD, but it is not DISTANCE, IT IS DIFFERENCE. Only through SALVATION can my UNLIKENESS be turned into HIS LIKENESS, which is so GREAT.

IT IS TIME TO RE-EXAMINE OUR CONDITION

In view of recent happenings, it would be to our benefit to take a deep, clear look—deep into the PRESENT CONDITION OF OUR SOUL. Crisis time can be very helpful in looking at ourselves, for life has a way of lulling us into a FALSE STATE OF BEING. Business as usual has surely taken a great toll on many folks who enjoy the UNINTERRUPTED LIFE that seems to be so prevalent. It is so easy for all of us to just ROCK ALONG and never take a GOOD HARD LOOK INTO OURSELVES. Maybe a few PENETRATING QUESTIONS are in order, for to my way of thinking, BEING LOST is not really an OPTION.

I am very concerned with the very scary attitude I sense among us, "ONCE SAVED ALWAYS SAVED." While none of you would dare shout this out among your peers, from the standpoint of various actions of late, I am feeling like many of you are now embracing such FOLLY. I say that with a desire for the best in your lives, not with any type of desire to be UNKIND. I have watched very carefully and have noticed some SIGNS that have now DISTURBED ME. The GREAT LACK of concern for the LOST, the almost FLIPPANT ATTITUDE about SIN, LOOSE MORALS AND LIVING. I have been very bothered by so many among us who NEVER PRAY BEFORE SERVICE OR SELDOM PRAY AT THE ALTAR SERVICE. There has been an increase in the AMOUNT OF CHURCH MISSED as if it has now become NO BIG DEAL. Many of you have been very DISHONEST ABOUT TITHING AND GIVING; this is still, to me, A SPIRITUAL INDICATOR of the WORST KIND.

I feel we have now entered into the very beginnings of SORROWS, that we are marching rapidly toward the WORLD DISASTERS predicted in both DANIEL AND REVELATIONS. I am really PLEADING with all: take INVENTORY OF YOUR SOUL'S CONDITION. If JESUS CAME TODAY WOULD YOU BE READY TO GO?

SALVATION IS PERSONAL; SO IS OUR RESPONSIBILITY

We would all agree that being SAVED was not designed by JESUS to be an assembly line–type experience, although we can surely point to the various requirements; REPENTANCE, BAPTISM AND RECEIVING THE HOLY GHOST. To be BORN FROM ABOVE must be the GREATEST EXPERIENCE available to any person, to actually have GOD ALMIGHTY take up HIS RESIDENCE within our frame is so GLORIOUS. To think that GOD wants to be so close to us, to live within our bodies, to be affecting all our ways, makes it SO PERSONAL.

I am very concerned with the current wave of ideas that tend to DISMISS THE PERSON from being PERSONALLY RESPONSIBLE for the maintaining of the SPIRITUAL LEVEL OF LIVING. Somehow folks seem to think that getting saved or being born again is all that is involved for their part, but we are told many things with regard to our SALVATION. These seem to be our job, and not HIS;

- KEEP YOURSELVES IN THE LOVE OF GOD,
- PRESENT YOUR BODIES A LIVING SACRIFICE,
- SUBMIT YOURSELVES TO THOSE OVER YOU,
- WALK IN THE SPIRIT, LIVE IN THE SPIRIT,
- FIGHT THE GOOD FIGHT OF FAITH,
- MORTIFY YOUR MEMBERS ON THE EARTH,
- SET YOUR AFFECTIONS ON THINGS ABOVE,
- PURSUE HOLINESS—WITHOUT WHICH NO ONE CAN SEE THE LORD,
- BE YE THANKFUL, BE FAITHFUL, BE LOYAL TO HIM,
- COMMIT TO JESUS WHAT WE WANT KEPT FOREVER,

- HONOR THE LORD WITH THE FIRST FRUITS OF YOUR SUBSTANCE,
- GIVE AND IT SHALL BE GIVEN TO YOU,
- HUMBLE YOURSELF BEFORE GOD DAILY,
- DO NOT BE A SOWER OF DISCORD AMONG BRETHREN,
- RUN YOUR RACE WITH PATIENCE,
- PROVIDE FOR THOSE OF YOUR OWN FAMILY,
- FORGIVE AND YE SHALL BE FORGIVEN.

These are a few things God demands of those of us who have been saved, we must continue in the WAY OF TRUTH until the END.

GO TO THE ANT
AND LEARN OF HIS WAYS

The above statement comes from Prov 6:6 and challenges the SLUGGARD to study the little ant and learn something that would help that lazy person to CHANGE. If we read the rest of the challenge, it becomes quite obvious that THE ANT is anything but WELFARE-MINDED OR EVEN LAID BACK; THEY ARE VERY INDUSTRIOUS. The ant colony is quite complex and organized, God has somehow put within this little creature an awareness regarding THE FUTURE and also THE NEED FOR EACH ANT TO DO THE JOB ASSIGNED if the colony is to survive and fulfill its place in creation. I pray that all reading this little article would become more aware that each of us has been put where we are for a definite purpose, and to fail in our task has far reaching implications.

NO ONE CAN LIVE UNTO THEMSELVES, NOR DOES FAILING TO DO OUR JOB NOT REALLY MATTER. Each and every one of us HAS VALUE and certain things God expects us to do, STRIFE AND JEALOUSY need not show their ugly faces among us. I cannot do what some folks can do, in fact I cannot do everything nor even many things very well. I can by the GRACE OF GOD, do the JOB ASSIGNED to me by my CREATOR GOD and bring to HIM, HONOR OF GLORY. POTENTIALS are given to each of us, GOD has not failed to grant each of HIS WORKS some SPECIFIC CAPABILITY and HE does not hold any of us ACCOUNTABLE for what we can't do, we must come to KNOW OUR ABILITIES and function there.

I am not worried because I am limited in various areas. I will give myself to flowing in my field and pray for JESUS to help me be the best for HIM ALONE. I wish at times I could be more talented and gifted, but I refuse to FRUSTRATE MYSELF over that, I can DO SOMETHING AND THAT IS WHAT I MUST DO.

Now ask yourself, "WHAT CAN I DO to help this CHRISTIAN COLONY be better?" And then do it. You're a SAINT, not a SLUGGARD!

KEEP THY HEART, LIFE'S ISSUES FLOW OUT

The writer of the PROVERBS challenges all humanity to KEEP OUR HEARTS WITH ALL DILIGENCE, FOR OUT OF THE HEART ARE THE ISSUES OF LIFE. This HUMAN ORGAN is the key to the health level for our flesh. I wonder just what kind of impact our SPIRITUAL HEARTS must play in our lives? We are told to be very interested about our INNER SELVES, OUR HEARTS if you please, for a number of reasons:

- Our heart is the center of our emotional selves.
- We feel, experience and give out from within the HEART.
- We are told to LOVE THE LORD WITH ALL OF OUR HEARTS, with all our emotional parts.
- To get saved we MUST BELIEVE WITH OUR HEARTS.
- Blessed are the PURE IN HEART, for they shall see GOD, for our GOD wants us, NOT OUR STUFF.

While it is very important that we have a change of mind and habits when we come to the LORD, we must also experience a DRASTIC HEART CHANGE, FOR WITH THE HEART expression for our GREAT GOD is demonstrated. Love and affection must flow out of our HEARTS and not just our HEADS. JESUS loves us with a PERFECT LOVE and desires that we LOVE HIM IN RETURN from the depths of our inner being. We must be on guard about what the enemy tries to put within our hearts, FOR OUT OF THE ABUNDANCE OF THE HEART, THE MOUTH SPEAKETH. The OVERFLOW will be REVEALED through our lips first and then our lives. The heart we are told is DECEITFUL ABOVE ALL THINGS AND DESPERATELY WICKED, WHO CAN KNOW IT?

Only our LORD can really know what is inside of all of us, so we must cry out like DAVID and say; SEARCH ME O LORD AND KNOW MY HEART and LEAD ME IN YOUR PATHS, TRY ME, PURGE ME.

THE GREAT BLESSING OF FEELING SO BAD

I know the title of this article seems a little strange, but please listen to my tale. I recently was caught in a situation that I had tried so hard to avoid and due to someone else, I ended up the BAD GUY. I talked with the offended one and made my sincere apology for the episode and yet all the while I felt SO TERRIBLE, SO BAD. As my head cleared and my heart made an honest search, I realized that the BAD FEELING was really a SIGN of an HONEST HEART that had not wanted the problem, and that deep within me I had truly wanted WHAT WAS RIGHT AND FAIR.

The fact it had not turned out properly was not my doing, but I still was made to feel TERRIBLE, offering my statements of sorrow to which I was quickly told all was O.K. I guess I think that God allows us into situations not of our making and even permits the wrong to become ours, yet I thank HIM for the BAD FEELINGS for they have borne witness that I AM NOT A DECEIVER OR ONE WHO DELIGHTS IN HURTING OTHERS. Now that I have been made to FEEL BAD, I am now starting to FEEL GLAD over FEELING BAD for I know deep inside NO EVIL INTENTION WAS BIRTHED from myself.

Have not some of you gone through times when someone you cared deeply for was hurt, OR you just misread something? And then you just FELT LIKE A HEEL and tried to correct the situation — even to the point of APOLOGY and requesting FORGIVENESS for the whole thing? Better to be very GLAD at times that you are able to FEEL AWFUL over various things; GOD IS STILL WORKING WITHIN YOU.

Our generation seems to have lost the ability to feel BAD, ASHAMED OR GUILTY. WE IN THE CHURCH MUST NOT LOSE THESE THINGS.

When we SIN, thank GOD for CONVICTION IF WE FAIL. Thank GOD for something within that feels SORROW yet desires to be better. I AM GLAD TO FEEL BAD OVER SOME THINGS SO I can do what is needed to become GLAD AGAIN.

GIVING THANKS IN THE MIDST OF WHATEVER

This holiday time finds our nation in the midst of a mess. Many are dead in the attacks by terrorists, our army is now fighting in a foreign land, many of our home folks have been put out of work, the stock market has hurt many investors, the threat of chemical sickness and death is very real; YET IN THE MIDST OF ALL THIS, WE CAN, AND SHOULD, OFFER THANKS TO GOD.

Our faith is not rooted in circumstances, but in the BLOODY CROSS; our hope is not coming from earth, but from our RISEN LORD REIGNING IN THE HEAVENS. Our present situation may leave much to be desired, but our situation is not FINAL, it is what Paul calls TEMPORAL, WHICH IS SUBJECT TO CHANGE, but GOD who has called us and has so wonderfully blessed us, CANNOT CHANGE. We need to be THANKFUL IN THE MIDST OF OUR VARIOUS MESSED UP AREAS for HIS FAITHFUL AND GRACIOUS dealings with all of us.

Paul was aboard a storm-tossed vessel with darkness and possible death ahead, but HE GAVE THANKS in the MIDST OF THE STORM and so impacted the other folks they too GAVE THANKS, ATE AND WERE SPARED. Daniel was facing possible death, but in the MIDST OF DANGER he opened the window and PRAYED, PRAISED AND GAVE THANKS. His deliverance flowed from an attitude of THANKSGIVING— ANGELS were released into the MIDST OF HIS MESS over THANKSGIVING offered in the face of forces seeking to STOP HIM FROM TALKING WITH HIS GOD.

Paul and Silas had been beaten and treated terribly, but at midnight they PRAYED, SANG PRAISES—which is actually OFFERING THANKS, and into THE MIDST OF THE MESS, God moved and SALVATION for the prison guard was experienced. OH THE AWESOME POWER OF JUST GIVING THANKS IN THE MIDST OF OUR MESS. Who can tell what may happen or who may come into the KINGDOM over any one of us GIVING THANKS IN OUR PRESENT MESS?

IT IS THAT TIME OF THE YEAR AGAIN

The time has come again for the human race to get into the giving, buying and cheering mood. We have just come through THANKSGIVING and are rushing into the CHRISTMAS SEASON and many feelings seem to arise that must be dealt with. My mailbox has had a load of letters full of APPEALS from every sort of needy group and, I am sure, most are very honorable. The FEELING that has attacked me as I DAILY deal with these REQUESTS is simply this, NOT ANOTHER ONE; MAN, DON'T THEY EVER GET ENOUGH MONEY? I CANNOT GIVE TO EVERY ONE! Even the letters seem longer and the photos are more moving. Although it can be very FRUSTRATING, NEEDS DO NOT TAKE HOLIDAYS and HUNGER DOES NOT READ CALENDAR DATES.

I feel it can be very easy to just SHUT OUR EYES, CLOSE OUR HEARTS AND HIDE OUR OFTEN OPENED WALLETS due to the constant requests. The news has been reporting that many organizations are feeling the PINCH due to the September 11 episode and I wonder if THE WORK OF GOD WILL ALSO SUFFER AT THIS TIME? May God help all of us to keep our FOCUS on the right things, which must ever be the LOST, HURTING AND NEEDFUL OF SPIRITUAL TRUTHS AND EXPERIENCE.

Even though we have been through the recent towers tragedy, we still are BLESSED FOLKS and still have more than most countries. Please consider a GIFT FOR CHRIST this season, something we could send off into the work for the establishing of new works that will help SOULS TO BE SAVED. I know that most of you already are planning to spend on kids, grand kids, husbands, wives, and others; ANY PLANS FOR GIVING TO THE ONE WHO MADE THE SEASON A REALITY?

Stay THANKFUL and the SPIRIT OF GIVING will come easier to you, SPEND SOMETHING FOR ETERNITY and you will REAP ETERNALLY.

TIPS FOR CELEBRATING CHRISTMAS WISELY

CHRISTMAS IS THE MOST SPECIAL SEASON. It can be ruined with STRESS AND PAIN or enjoyed realizing the following truths:

1. KEEP JESUS IN THE CENTER OF CHRISTMAS. Grasp the SIGNIFICANCE of the INCARNATION. Jn 1;14, 2 Cor 5;19, Hebs 1;1–3, 2 Tim 3;16. Our best and most lasting memories should be FAMILY, FRIENDS, CHURCH SERVICES, MUSIC AND WORSHIP; NOT SHOPPING, BUYING, STUFF.

2. DON'T BE MANIPULATED BY COMMERCIALISM. GIVING GIFTS should be our personal expressions of LOVE, CARE AND APPRECIATION; not from a sense of GUILT OR BEING FORCED TO—so such–and-such won't be upset...Don't spend money you cannot spare.

3. SUICIDE, HOMICIDE AND PSYCHIATRIC PROBLEMS always increase during this season. WHY? Our culture is so impacted by the tyranny of "things," we are forced to stretch budgets. A CLIMATE OF GREED AND GUILT operates and causes some to feel CHEAP for not giving, and others to feel LEFT OUT for not receiving.

4. SPEND TIME WITH FRIENDS AND FAMILY AS AN OCCASION FOR ENJOYMENT, NOT as a trial of forced ENDURING. PEOPLE MATTER, NOT STUFF. Use the season as a means to REACH OUT, TO TOUCH SOME LIVES in a LASTING WAY.

5. ALLOW CHRISTMAS TO BE A TIME FOR OUR COMING TOGETHER, NOT COMING APART. Many folks have differing convictions about the decorations, gift giving, trees, etc., so act wisely.

6. FINISH THE OLD YEAR AND PREPARE FOR THE NEW ONE. Close out the year with a great gift idea—A CLEAR CONSCIENCE. Assess GOALS: did you reach any? Determine what must be done to reach them in the New Year. Repent of all MISSED OPPORTUNITIES or LACK OF INVOLVEMENT. DETERMINE TO BE A BETTER CHRISTIAN.

DON'T BEMOAN WHAT THIS WORLD IS COMING TO. REALIZE WHAT AND WHO CAME TO THIS WORLD. GOD IS THE GREATEST GIVER—HOW ABOUT HIS KIDS?

THAT YE WALK WORTHY OF THE LORD

All of us will agree I am sure that none of we SAVED FOLKS feel worthy of being SAVED, and are sometimes so overwhelmed with what God has done for us. We all know where He brought us from, but I wonder if we really consider our proper response to SO GREAT A SALVATION? God does not ask any of us to be SUPERMAN in the life we live, but rather that with HONEST HEARTS and DILIGENT SPIRITUAL DESIRES, WE WOULD SEEK to WALK WORTHY of the LORD.

When I recall how I came out of darkness into light, how Jesus totally forgave my horrible past and how He filled me with the HOLY GHOST. How could I just sit and coast along as if I had nothing to do? God could have just as easily passed me by and talked to my neighbors, but in HIS GRACE, He called me out—into and for. I must therefore JUSTIFY HIS GOODNESS with a LIFE THAT HONORS HIS GOODNESS. I do feel a great OBLIGATION TO WALK WORTHY, but often I seem to fall, fail and just flop. But the SAME GOD who GRACED ME at the start stands so ready to RECEIVE ME AND REFRESH ME AND RESTORE ME if I will just be totally honest with HIM.

Some of the folks who attend this assembly and call themselves HIS KIDS give to me the impression that JESUS IS TOO HARSH, DEMANDING, OR WHATEVER. If a call to change some area of their lives goes out, they take offense and take to pointing to some others who live the same as some type of JUSTIFICATION. Another response to being asked to adjust something will be to check with RELATIVES that don't live like us, or even worse, talk with folks who have now left this assembly, NOW PASTORING THEMSELVES. This way of doing things seems to me an INSULT to the GREAT GOD OF GLORY.

Why would anyone seem to experience SALVATION and then do all they can NEVER TO SELL OUT, DESIRE HOLINESS, WANT TO WIN THE LOST, MAKE SURE CHURCH SERVICES NEVER INTERFERE WITH VARIOUS SOCIAL SCHEDULES and MAKE SURE GOD WILL NEVER COME FIRST except in their way of interpretation? May God help all of us to WANT TO WALK WORTHY FOR JESUS SAKE.

WE HAVE BEEN VISITED FROM ANOTHER WORLD

I realize the title of my little thought seems to be like some SCI–FI story, but the truth is, ANOTHER WORLD penetrated our darkness and paid us a ROYAL VISIT in the FORM OF A LITTLE BABY. We must take some time during this GREAT SEASON and really think about the WHY and the WHO of this visit. We were in great trouble with our SINS, our jailer was SATAN, the chances of escape were none. Our future would be as BLEAK as our past and present, yet GOD SO LOVED US (regardless of being the WORST TYPE OF REBELS AND RUNNING WITH THE VILEST REBEL OF ALL TIME) GOD WANTED ALL OF US TO COME HOME INTO HIS HEART.

The truth of what I have just written needs to PENETRATE DEEPLY into our understanding as well as our emotions. We were HELD CAPTIVE and yet GOD WANTS US GIVEN FREEDOM, WOW…To think that we were SO LOVED and DESIRED BY DEITY…it should HUMBLE all of us. Knowing so many hidden things regarding our own lives and personalities might make these TRUTHS seem a little FAR–FETCHED, but TRUTH is often STRANGER THAN FICTION.

The issue of the CHRISTMAS VISITATION must never be "our terrible condition," but rather HIS GREAT GRACE AND LOVE: for the book says, "FOR GOD SO LOVED THE WORLD" (not just nice folks, but NASTY, SELFISH, SINNING people like us). Why HE CAME is really not the issue. The fact that HE CHOSE TO COME should evoke such THANKS AND PRAISE, WE SHOULD BE ABLE TO DROWN OUT THE BEST OF CHOIRS WITH OUR GRATEFUL VOICES. Say it to yourself now, "HE CAME ABOUT ME, HE LOVES ME, HE WANTS ME TO COME HOME TO HIS HEART, HE HOLDS NO ANIMOSITY

TOWARDS ME, HE IS THE REASON FOR THE SEASON."

I pray during the next few days of festivity that we will all take some time to REFLECT, REHEARSE AND REJOICE over this GREAT VISITATION from the HEAVENS and the LEADER HIMSELF. I am glad to–the–bone for HIS ARRIVAL and for the GREAT WORK that was accomplished while He was here.

MERRY CHRISTMAS!

THE NEED AND BLESSING OF LOOKING BACKWARD

It has come once again; the end of a year and the hope of a brand new one, it surely is time to LOOK OVER OUR SHOULDERS and RECOUNT what GOD has done, what we have accomplished and also what we have failed to follow through with. We all can shout aloud that God has been so very good to all of us, PRAYERS HE HAS ANSWERED, SITUATIONS HE TOOK US THROUGH, TIMES WE FAILED TERRIBLY, YET WE FOUND FRESH MERCY, CHALLENGES THAT THE HOLY GHOST HAS PRESENTED TO OUR HEARTS IN SECRET TIMES OF WAITING. I know our church family has gone through many things that might have been disastrous, but GOD HAS BEEN FAITHFUL. We have said FAREWELL to some FINE SAINTS and FRIENDS, and have also had NEW BABIES arrive. We have been part of some WEDDINGS as well as some sad separations, yet THE GOOD HAS WONDERFULLY OUTWEIGHED THE BAD.

As we all stand on the brink of a new year, may all of us REFLECT on our FINANCES, how well have we done, for nothing is actually ours—we are STEWARDS OF HIS GIFTS, TIME, MONEY AND TALENTS. I know from being pastor, some need to REALLY REPENT AND RESTORE what has been either misused or just not used for the work of GOD. Please RE-EVALUATE your PRAYER LIFE. Have you GAINED OR LOST ground? How about ATTENDANCE, NOT JUST TO REGULAR SERVICES, HOW about the SPECIAL MEETINGS AND SPEAKERS that our assembly has been so blessed to have visit us?

COULD YOU MEET GOD TODAY WITH THE RECORD OF YOUR GIVING, LIVING AND SACRIFICE this past year? Please hear me, I am not trying to be UNKIND, but rather trying to get all of us to REFLECT

UPON OUR LIVES, REPENT OF AREAS THAT WE HAVE FAILED AND DETERMINE by GRACE to do better with the upcoming UNSOILED YEAR. I want to THANK so many who have been so deeply involved, very faithful to so many things, to all who have prayed for me, giving over and over while others did not, MAY GOD BLESS YOU. BE ENCOURAGED, THE GOD WHO BROUGHT US THIS FAR WILL SURELY GO WITH US THIS NEW YEAR.... May this year 2002 find all of us holier for Him.

ABOVE ALL, I MUST BE SAVED AT ALL COST

As we begin this New Year full of grand possibility and hidden treasures, MAY GOD challenge each of us with what is the most important work for each of us: WE MUST BE SAVED. You may feel that this challenge is not needed, but as the PASTOR and WATCHMAN, my heart is greatly disturbed over so many things that are JUST NOT RIGHT. We all must take time and REFLECT on what we had promised to do and have not, how we purposed to do this or that, to become more CHRIST LIKE and SEEK THE KINGDOM OF GOD FIRST and have not. It is so easy for any of us to get so BUSY WITH LIFE that we fail to MAKE A REAL LIFE, for nothing is as PRECIOUS AS THE SOUL.

I can imagine that some of you reading this will quickly discard or disregard my effort, but PLEASE listen to me a few moments; we are all going BEFORE THE LORD and GIVING AN ACCOUNT, not only of DEEDS AND MISDEEDS, but also of WASTED TIME, SELF-FIRST SYNDROME, WASTED FUNDS, LACK OF LOYALTY, FAILURE TO SACRIFICE ACCORDING TO OUR MEANS, UNWILLINGNESS TO GET INVOLVED IN ALL WE COULD HAVE, PRAYERLESS DAYS AND NITES, LACK OF STUDY OF THE WORD, THE LACK OF PASSION FOR THE LOST, BEING SO HIT-AND-MISS WITH CHURCH ATTENDANCE, the list could go on and on. When we think of WHAT JESUS DID FOR US AT CALVARY, OF THE GREAT SALVATION WE HAVE EXPERIENCED, THE HORDES OF LOST SOULS WE ARE RESPONSIBLE FOR REACHING…how can any of us just live such SLOPPY LIVES?

IF YOU ARE TODAY WHAT YOU HAVE ALWAYS BEEN, YOU ARE PROBABLY NOT EVEN SAVED, for with GOD, growth and progress and conformity to HIS IMAGE ARE TO BE NORMAL OCCURRENCES. I pray none of us keep living from MEMORY or from PREVIOUS PERFORMANCES. We all must be ANOINTED WITH FRESH OIL if we are going to DO HIS WONDERFUL WILL AND BE READY FOR HIS APPEARING. If the life you are living is NATURAL only, ask God for the SUPERNATURAL.

THE BLESSING OF BEING A BETHANY TO JESUS

Most of us know that BETHANY was not a person, but a place; but we can learn some wonderful lessons from the PEOPLE who made the PLACE precious to JESUS. Mary and Martha lived there with their brother Lazarus, but something seemed to exist there that seemed to draw JESUS again and again. He seemed to find an atmosphere in that home and those three people that MINISTERED TO HIM in such a way–he was refreshed and relaxed there. I want to be that kind of person, creating the type of place JESUS is drawn to, and delights to come there.

I wonder if we can ever really grasp how much GOD desires to be with us, to just sit with us and ENJOY OUR COMPANY? He has gone on record many times telling us about HIS HEART'S DESIRE to DWELL AMONG MEN, He seems to take great pleasure just being with HIS CREATION: MAN....

I have often told you and others, I believe JESUS IS IN LOVE WITH ME; but I wonder if we have ever considered HOW MUCH HE WANTS TO BE WITH US? I know there were differences that existed in that home, two very different personalities, yet both found a wonderful way of making JESUS both warm and welcomed. I am sure I have missed many chances to have HAD JESUS as my guest because of various actions, attitudes or just plain SELFISHNESS, so HE was forced to seek serenity elsewhere. As the lady in the BIBLE who built a little chamber for the PROPHET, I want to prepare a place for MY LORD to want to come to...how about you?

May GOD help each of us to look into our hearts and homes and deal with anything that would make JESUS not want to stop by and visit with us OFTEN. I am one that desires HIS PERSON and not just HIS GIFTS, I want HIM to take PLEASURE when HE thinks about me, for HE has so few places and persons that afford HIM REST AND JOY.

THE NEED FOR AND BLESSING OF RENDING

The book of Isaiah cries out to God saying, "OH, THAT THOU WOULD REND THE HEAVENS AND COME DOWN." There comes to all of our lives that deep longing for the GOD OF GLORY to just rip apart any barrier between HIM and us and just show forth HIS GLORY. To REND is to tear apart, to rip with a violence, to split in two as a tree is by some lightning. There are three rendings we need to see.

"REND YOUR HEARTS and not your clothes," was the cry from JOEL. It seems much easier to just rip the clothing in some type of anguish, rather than to REND THE HEART. This is really a call to DEEP REPENTANCE, not just a form, but a real tearing apart of the heart in violent contrition. We seem to cry for a MOVING OF GOD, but I know that without A RENT HEART we will not experience a RENDING OF THE HEAVENS.

The VEIL was rent when JESUS DIED, but that fabric didn't tear apart until our WONDERFUL LORD JESUS had his own heart rent. His heart surely came apart with the tragedy of our sins, the brutal treatment received at CALVARY, his HEART RUPTURED on the TREE for us.... Following HIS RENT HEART, THE VEIL WAS RENT which in turn allowed PENTECOST TO HAPPEN. I believe the HEAVENS WERE RENT as the HOLY GHOST CAME DOWN, God tore in two the last barrier to our BLESSING OF HIS SPIRIT. The same must happen again; we must REND OUR HEARTS SO THAT GOD WILL REND THE HEAVENS AND COME DOWN in fullness of SPIRITUAL POWER.

We ALONE hold the key and GOD ALONE can REND THE HEAVENS. SO let us do our part and God will surely do HIS PART, WE MUST CONFESS TO POSSESS.

DANIEL WEBSTER WEPT OVER THE QUESTION

The great statesman was asked one time what had been the greatest thought he had go through his GREAT BRAIN? Mr. Webster was so moved by the question, he actually ran out of the building weeping and sobbing. After regaining himself, he reentered the building and answered with this reply, "the most profound question is simply this; I AM RESPONSIBLE FOR THE SPIRITUAL WELL-BEING FOR MY FELLOW MAN. I WILL BE HELD ACCOUNTABLE AS RESPONSIBLE TO MY GOD FOR MY LIFE, MY ACTIONS AND FOR THE GOSPEL." Please here it again; WHAT HAS BEEN THE MOST PROFOUND THOUGHT YOU HAVE EVER HAD MR. WEBSTER? WITH TEARS STREAMING AND BODY NOW TREMBLING–MY RESPONSIBILITY TO MY GOD...

While we constantly must be on guard about the WORLD, SATAN AND SIN, I think today we are being beaten badly with the terrible spirit of INDIFFERENCE, APATHY AND LACK OF RESPONSIBILITY. It seems so easy for all of us to attend church if we do not have some OTHER PRESSING APPOINTMENT, to throw some change or few dollars into the plate–but not AS SACRIFICIAL, to applaud when the need to reach the LOST is shouted, but NEVER TO SHOW UP AND GET INVOLVED. How long has it been since some of you have REALLY WEPT over the LOST, or BEEN MOVED to a place of total frustration and disgust about the LACK OF PASSION AND CONCERN?

I know I am before the LORD DAILY, asking for a FRESH TOUCH deep within my soul that would IMPACT THE WAY I LIVE, FEEL AND PRAY. I am not speaking as one who has arrived, but rather from a platform of personal DISSATISFACTION and a DRIVE to become WHAT HE CALLED ME TO BECOME. Have you thought about what we will tell the LORD

JESUS when we are asked, WHAT DID YOU DO WITH ALL THE TIME AND MONEY I allowed you to have, What kind of involvement consumed both time and money, did you share the BREAD OF LIFE with many, any, none? May God help us to lift up our eyes and behold the harvest.

GIVE ME CHILDREN, LEST I DIE

Rachel pleaded with Jacob about having some offspring, but she was rebuffed by her husband for he had no power to do what she requested; ONLY GOD COULD FIX THIS. I know that God did remember her cry and did bless her with children, but not until she had reached the place of DESPERATION. I think that many of us who really desire various things from God in our lives fail to experience them over just one area of lack – DESPERATION. We must somehow become DESPERATE AND DANGEROUS in order to receive some things from God.

I know we have been told to ASK, SEEK and KNOCK, but in all fairness, many of us do not BECOME DESPERATE about getting the answers we want. It seems that often we are like the king who was told to smite his arrows and he stopped at three, at which the prophet became angry. If we realized how many spirits are arrayed against us daily and how often God wanted to grant us the needed abilities to accomplish the tasks, we would surely become DESPERATE. I remember the story of the four lepers and how one decided just SITTING AND DYING was not an option, so he got up and tried something else, which caused the three others to go with him.

God wants us to believe, but also to become INTENSE and DRIVEN so we cannot be refused. We do the same thing with our own children, friends or associates when they approach us. A DESPERATE APPEAL usually will affect us quite differently than some pathetic plea as if the solution was no big deal. What do you want from God that you DESPERATELY must have? Is there a GIFT you WANT, A SITUATION that needs an answer now? Is there some area of weakness that must be whipped? I know that our GREAT LORD JESUS can tell the DIFFERENCE in our cries just like a mother can when her child cries out. I want to bear fruit for JESUS, I don't want to waste the gift of time doing stuff that will not cause me to have some sheaves for HIM. I want new life working in me and through me, how about you?

THE POWER AND NEED TO BE FERVENT IN SPIRIT

We believe that our LORD JESUS was GOD in a flesh body, but I wonder if we ever grasp how HIS PASSION as a man allowed the SPIRIT WITHIN to flow out from HIS BODY. To be FERVENT is to be HOT, GLOWING, BURNING, TO BE INTENSELY DEVOTED, TO BE PASSIONATE. No wonder Paul told us to be FERVENT IN SPIRIT, SERVING THE LORD, for JESUS is worth us being INFUSED WITH FIRE AND PASSION. We must now remember how HE BURNED WITH PASSION for the work of REDEMPTION and that the terrible price of CALVARY, REJECTION AND RIDICULE were not barriers to him.

There is not really much of any consequence that ever happens without some type of FERVENCY behind it. Somehow we must ask our LORD to infuse our hearts beyond our heads so that PASSION will drive us rather than REASON hinder us. There are many things with GOD that surpass reason, but are fueled by FERVENCY AND PASSION. I know that many folks who used to serve the LORD JESUS used to have a FERVENT HEART, but seemingly have either lost that, or just in living life, have allowed other things to TAKE OUT THE SIZZLE FROM THEIR SOULS. We must become FERVENT like ELIJAH was in his day, ANGRY WITH THE FALSE AND GREATLY ZEALOUS for the NAME OF HIS GOD. To be just upset at wrong and not passionate about the right makes us not much better than the PROTESTER WITH A PLACARD.

Only by having GREAT PASSIONS can we ever really lift the SOUL TO GREAT THINGS. We must be MOVED WITH MERCY and CARE DEEPLY to the point that PERSONAL NEEDS are laid aside so that the GOAL can be reached. Why should some ATHLETE be driven to something while the APOSTOLICS ARE LED BY APATHY?

I know that to be A PASSIONATE PERSON will cost much PAIN IN OUR DEEP SOULS, but that is a small price if through A FERVENT SPIRIT God is glorified, the lost spared and the church EDIFIED.

MOVED WITHIN, BUT UNMOVED WITHOUT

I wonder how many times we all have been touched and really moved within by a story, a song or sermon and yet, we have not been moved into action. Most of us know some measure of TRUTH, but I am concerned regarding our UNCONCERN to seemingly DO NOTHING ABOUT WHAT WE KNOW. One writer tells us, "to KNOW TO DO GOOD AND NOT DO IT," IS SIN, so to be aware of something either required or needful–and not do it, becomes sin to all of us.

To become SAVED does not end the story, we must become changed in every area of our walk, to BELIEVE AND NOT BEHAVE is to INSULT the GREAT SALVATION we claim to have experienced. All face various areas of our lives that seem to either RESIST CHANGE or IGNORE THE NEED TO. A bad habit must be replaced only with a good one; thought will not accomplish the job, ACTION IS REQUIRED. Sometimes I feel we are counting on the SERMON to do it for us, or even the SERVICE. While both are needful, neither can of themselves change us, we alone must make the right choices and then back them up with the appropriate actions. It is so easy to be moved and then go out from the church building and LIVE UNMOVED. Our witness falters and the world that watches must be very perplexed by MIXED SIGNALS being received from the redeemed.

The story in Judges 5, regarding the REUBENITES should help us: it states that they were moved by great reasonings and searchings in their hearts over the CRISIS, but they still managed to STAY AWAY FROM THE BATTLE. While they seemed so concerned, their conduct was SHAMEFUL. How are we doing?

USER FRIENDLY OR ALMIGHTY GOD FRIENDLY

Today we are being bombarded with the constant jargon of things being user friendly, making things very compatible and comfortable to people. This has now spilled, or should I say SPEWED, over into the church where leaders are being daily challenged by a SIN LOVING, SELF LOVING society not to require much of them. I want you to know that all of us stand in need of DELIVERANCE and even the most liberal folks would shout AMEN.

The real problem is the SECOND PHASE OF DELIVERANCE which also must be experienced by all the FRESHLY EMANCIPATED, which is becoming DISCIPLES, DISCIPLINED ONES. That second CROSS is the one that has given birth to so many CHURCH GROUPS, STUDY GROUPS AND NON-DENOMINAL FOLKS. We are being forced to deal with a society that is being sold a BILL OF GOODS that will not stand up in the face of CHRIST, OR HIS WORD. Jesus did not die for me, you, or anyone else so we could be FREE TO SIN, TO STAY THE SAME, OR SIMPLY REFUSE TO DENY OUR SINFUL SELVES.

I believe all of us come to God with much surplus baggage and have never really understood what God intended when He so wonderfully LIBERATED US. To hear some folks talk, God is permitted to save them and then the SAME SPIRIT is told to just simply BUTT OUT of the rest of their lives. I know of a truth; THE HOLY GHOST was given to lead and guide us into ALL TRUTH and our BEING CONFORMED INTO HIS IMAGE was all part of the original deal, although most of said saved folks do not agree…

To be blessed with the birth of a child is great, but to leave that little bundle of potential to DO AS IT PLEASES would be CRIMINAL, AND YET THIS IS WHAT MODERN BELIEVERS are being told is the way it should be. We must allow the SPIRIT to speak into our lives, pointing out areas to be dealt with, may God help us to be both DELIVERED AND DISCIPLINED.

GOD WANTS US TO EXPERIENCE DOUBLE REST

Jesus told us to come unto Him and find that He would GIVE US REST. The sinner may seek rest, bury themselves in all types of sin and activity, but there is really no REST FOR THE WICKED SAITH THE LORD. He tells us the WICKED are like the TROUBLED SEA that cannot REST, but stirs up all types of junk and trash from below the surface.

When anyone comes to JESUS, that person is looking for rest from the TASKMASTER OF SIN, driven on into ENDLESS SITUATIONS. I really am THANKFUL for the INITIAL REST we can and do find in CONFESSING AND FORSAKING OUR SINS AND SINFUL WAYS. The first rest offered is actually a REFRESHING FROM THE TOILS OF SIN AND THE HEAVY LOAD WE ARE FORCED TO CARRY. Jesus didn't mean for it to be a final place to abide, but rather a first step that would allow a more rich and permanent rest to occur.

The FIRST REST follows the word COME, we must respond with our heavy hearts and bleeding souls. To me, it is a PICTURE OF SALVATION, coming by faith unto JESUS and FORSAKING SIN AND SELF at HIS FEET. His PRECIOUS BLOOD gives REST THROUGH OUR REPENTANCE, but this first work is not FINAL, ONLY FIRST.

The second REST offered is found when any person willing TAKES HIS YOKE UPON THEM. This REST IS DEEP, ABIDING and requires a lot more than JUST COMING, it involves our WILLING SUBMISSION TO HIS YOKE. This may be called and taught by some as BONDAGE, but it is really LIBERTY AND LIFE at the best level. It is walking with and talking with and working with JESUS, YOKED UP WITH HIM and LEARNING OF HIM DAILY. It involves our saying GOOD BYE to our rights and personal liberty; we call it CONSECRATION. JESUS does DEMAND TOTAL SUBMISSION. Which rest are you enjoying now?

HOW SHALL WE ESCAPE IF WE NEGLECT

Having spoken to our church family this past SUNDAY, I want to share a few more thoughts regarding the PRICE OF NEGLECTING things in our lives that should not be treated with NEGLECT. In Hebrews we are challenged with these words, "HOW SHALL WE ESCAPE IF WE NEGLECT SO GREAT A SALVATION?" The answer is very EASY and yet VERY TERRIFYING–THERE IS NO ESCAPE FROM THE SHAME, BLAME AND DAMNATION. God has in GRACE offered the GREATEST PLAN for WHOSOEVER WILLS to be SAVED AND BLESSED, and to disregard it will prove to be our total undoing.

To NEGLECT HIS HOLY OFFER IS TO tell God you and I are not impressed with it, we do not feel it is worth our time or money, and that we have come up with a better way to be saved from our sins. WHAT AN INSULT TO THE GLORY, MAJESTY AND GRACE of God in just offering any of us a CHANCE TO CHANGE. What kind of PUNISHMENT awaits any and all who DISREGARD the OFFER of the LIVING GOD, what will be done to us if we choose to NEGLECT the GREAT SALVATION that was purchased with the BLOOD OF JESUS THE LAMB OF GOD?

In Matthew 22, we are told of a man who came into the MARRIAGE FEAST, not having on the GARMENT provided for him by the host. We are told, "AND HE WAS SPEECHLESS," for he willingly HAD NEGLECTED to do as was the custom of that day. HE WAS CAST OUT INTO OUTER DARKNESS. Through idleness, slothfulness, the building decayeth and the house droppeth through, or falls apart. Do not NEGLECT to hear from HEAVEN, THE VOICE that calls unto us, for we are told soberly that we SHALL NOT ESCAPE. I am sure many who listened to me

Sunday have read into or out of the message through eyes and ears of bias. For this I am so sad; unwilling to accept the WORD and REPENT and REBUILD, some now have become CRITICS instead of HONEST HEARERS AND DOERS. Beware if you are NEGLECTING to CHANGE and PURSUE HOLINESS for we all will be judged by our LIGHT KNOWN.

THE BLESSING AND NEED OF REMEMBERING

No one feels good when they are seemingly overlooked, or some deed from them has now been FORGOTTEN. I read the other day from HIS GREAT WORD where God warned his people, "THOU SHALT REMEMBER THOU WAST A BONDMAN IN EGYPT AND A STRANGER." He told them to be kind to the STRANGER for you were once in the same fix, yet God showed kindness to you. Remembering can help us to defeat coldness of heart, indifference about another person's dilemma, for we were just like them in some degree.

SPIRITUAL DARKNESS follows on the heels of INDIFFERENCE AND BEING FORGETFUL of just how good our GOD HAS BEEN TO ALL OF US. Our fallen natures seem to retain the bad ability of not REMEMBERING JUST how lost and low we were when GRACE FOUND US. The fact that GOD LOVES US SO MUCH AND SO FREELY should cause the FLAME OF THANKFULNESS to burn very brightly. We need to recall often in our lives how rich and kind our GOD has been to us.

Remembering things from childhood can often bless us as well as cause feelings of hurt. Somehow, God has so put us together that, for the most part, we are able to block out many things and recall warm and good things. What God wanted then and now is that we all work at NOT FORGETTING how much we owe to GRACE and from that platform, show others the great works of GOD in our lives.

While we all should rejoice in our forgiven past, we still need to REMEMBER; at best, WE WERE THE SLAVES OF SATAN AND SIN. This will also protect us from ARROGANCE AND PRIDE. Our spirits need to REMEMBER that we didn't set ourselves free, but rather THE GREAT

GOD DID. Remembering also has the ability to make us THANKFUL and filled with PRAISE, for if it had not been for HIS GOODNESS, where would any of us be? May God help each of us to REMEMBER where we came from, what we were, and to break out in PRAISE.

HIMPOSSIBLE

Our lives are filled with situations and various people that challenge us to the depth of our souls and faith. All of us could point to things that seem to be JUST IMPOSSIBLE, but with GOD, ARE VERY POSSIBLE; WITH HIM, nothing can ever be IMPOSSIBLE. I am so glad we have a FRIEND that has all power and wisdom and wants us to WIN AT LIFE. I know I am very LIMITED in so many areas, but JESUS is not. All things are POSSIBLE WITH HIM; OR SIMPLY–HIMPOSSIBLE.

God seems to delight in allowing his kids to be put into situations that call for them to LOOK UNTO HIM for the fixing, answers or escape. Dependency does not sit well with AMERICAN THINKING, but GOD has his very own standards that He operates the entire world and universe by…. All through the Bible we are shown again and again in times of trouble, folks would TURN UNTO HIM to make the IMPOSSIBLE, POSSIBLE. The miracles of scripture reveal to us NOTHING IS IMPOSSIBLE WITH GOD, from dreaded diseases, difficult or dangerous situations; when people would call upon the GREAT GOD OF GLORY, that which seemed to them IMPOSSIBLE, SIMPLY BECAME POSSIBLE WITH HIM.

I am so glad that we do not have to fight alone, figure everything out on our own, or even walk through this tough world by ourselves. We have HIM with us, in us and coming again for us shortly. Whatever you are being FORCED TO FACE, turn from it just a moment and FACE HIM. After that LOOK OF FAITH, turn back to face the situation with the CONFIDENCE that this will not defeat me, destroy me, or in any way cause me to be lost. God loves me so much, cares about every detail of my life, and if I cast my cares upon HIM nothing shall be IMPOSSIBLE WITH HIM. Take it to HIM, leave it with HIM and believe HIM that nothing can DEFEAT HIM, for with HIM all things are surely POSSIBLE–IT REALLY IS HIMPOSSIBLE…

OUTLOOK ALWAYS HELPS DETERMINE OUTCOME

Often, situations we are forced to face and deal with can have their power to defeat taken away just by HOW WE LOOK AT THEM. Victory is often accomplished by the VISION we have of things. People who go around SOUR and SAD ARE LIVING REVELATIONS of some INWARD DISEASE that is really CONTROLLING them from the inside out. Negative folks seem to irritate many of us over their constant SAD–SACK approach to everything. Some things are just part of our lives, because we happen to be riding a PLANET CURSED BY SIN AND OUT OF CONTROL. Many of the issues we are confronted with just come with the turf, if SIN and SATAN were gone the irritations and problems would also be gone.

I personally make it my business to work on my attitude daily, my OUTLOOK carries great and far–reaching CONSEQUENCES. I cannot afford to have a sour view of life, LIFE IS A GIFT FROM GOD, various offensive things tied to the fine thing called LIFE are not HIS DOING. We all must battle against being some type of FATALIST who always sees the SKY FALLING and somehow must RUN FOR COVER. Surely the worst of us have enjoyed the rich flow of UPLIFT that has come to us from that grand person who has an ATTITUDE OF GRATITUDE. Thankful folks, believing folks and faith–filled folks seem to LIFT OUR SPIRITS, they reveal through their words and actions A TRUST IN GOD TO WORK THINGS OUT IN TIME.

The END RESULT of anything does not just happen, the law of sowing and reaping, of belief and behavior impact the final tally. I am sure if all of us gave ourselves more to studying the PROMISES and practicing the PRESENCE OF GOD, OUR OUTLOOKS would drastically change for the better. Regardless of what you are now dealing with, facing or suffering under, LIFT YOUR EYES UNTO THE HILLS, HELP IS ON THE WAY. He who called us to start this race will not fail us now, PURIFY YOUR OUTLOOK WITH A FRESH UPLOOK and you will ALTER YOUR OUTCOME…

TO STAND FOR GOD WE MUST PRACTICE KNEELING

I know many verses that shout loudly to us about STANDING, RESIST-ING AND FIGHTING, but I am totally convinced that all these positions flow out of the BEST POSITION for all of us, KNEELING. I feel that a position of KNEELING BEFORE GOD each day will enable the WEAKEST AND WORST of us to be able to STAND before the WORST PEOPLE and VILEST EVILS.

Our POWER WITHIN must come from ABOVE and to experience that, we must learn how to KNEEL. I know our society dreads, detests and despises any form of HUMILITY, CONTRITION, OR CONFESSION of weakness and sinfulness. Nevertheless, THE HOLY GOD we are serving has never been very IMPRESSED with what MAN LOVES AND HONORS. Contrary to the accepted norm, GOD LOVES HUMBLE FOLKS. He has gone on record–THE LORD RESISTS THE PROUD. He is attracted to HONEST KNEELING folks who know deep in their hearts, IF IT WERE NOT FOR GRACE AND MERCY, I would not even be here, or possibly be still alive.

I do not feel shameful or degraded when I KNEEL before the ALMIGHTY GOD and I am very glad that I can APPROACH HIS THRONE considering how vile and wicked I have been. I am very glad to bring my APPEAL while I KNEEL for it is just right, he is GOD, I am in NEED. I also want to tell all of you that I am totally convinced, HE IS WORTHY OF HONOR, FEAR AND RESPECT, for HE ALONE is GOD. To think we mortals, sinning folks could approach the SOVEREIGN of all the universe and ask for guidance, mercy, empowerment and grace to do HIS WILL.

I think that we all need to make the KNEELING POSITION our best one so that we will not have too far to fall whenever we are knocked down. KNEELING has another benefit; I can have COMPASSION on others who are hurting, pray better for all those who love to STAND ERECT and realize how KIND GOD HAS BEEN TO ME. Lets all, this week, KNEEL A LITTLE LONGER so we may then STAND A LOT LONGER–see you on the floor.

CONCEPT OR CONTACT— THEY ARE VERY DIFFERENT

Most people you meet possess some type of CONCEPT about God, Heaven, Hell, Judgment, Lifestyles, Church attendance and various other topics. The concern I have is that we, or many others, may have a CORRECT CONCEPT concerning GOD and yet never make CONTACT with HIM. We move in and through the world that HE GAVE to mankind, everything throbs with HIS SIGNATURE and yet, most people do not MAKE PERSONAL CONTACT with HIM. We can believe this or that, but CONTACT must follow SEEKING, FOR WE CANNOT JUST BUMP INTO HIM. There must come into our lives a DESIRE to really INTERACT with and make CONTACT with God, or it just will not happen.

I am very convinced that a large number of folks who attend WORSHIP SERVICES in various churches BELIEVE, PRAY, GIVE and yet have never made CONTACT in any depth of the word. There must be a level of FAITH, EXPECTATION and WILLINGNESS to quest after GOD, for He has chosen the medium of SELF REVELATION unto the HUNGRY AND THIRSTY. Bumping into the GOD OF GLORY, or believing it is some type of assumed automatic thing that just happens because we come here or go there, is wrong. What we all should do is SEEK GOD in such a way that HE would MANIFEST HIMSELF in an overwhelming way and allow us to make CONTACT.

The younger folks use the term, "CONNECTED," which means they met someone who they just were able to talk with or feel something about, so there was a CONNECTION MADE. We all have met folks we COULD NOT CONNECT with for some reason, but what a shame to BELIEVE IN GOD and yet in reality, never make a CONNECTION.

Ask yourself right now, "Am I making CONTACT, or am I just living by a CONCEPT?" THE RIGHT ANSWER CAN DETERMINE YOUR DESTINY. MAKE REAL CONTACT…

THE LORD IS A GOD OF CORRECT ORDER

One does not have to be a genius today to understand that our world is OUT OF ORDER. God, who went on record in the first book of the BIBLE, is ORDERLY AND EXACT. He began to correct the disaster and mess He found by putting various things into a PRECISE ORDER to allow fullness of function and purpose. The heavens themselves testify to the fact there is GREAT ORDER; the earth in the natural realm shouts the same. Nature flows from ORDER, seasons come and go, the winds and rains are servants unto the earth.

We can study various cycles that life forms go through, from the SWALLOW TO THE SALMON, THE BEAR AND THE BEE, all flow within a prescribed pattern and order. Only MAN is out of order, mankind is out of control and the reason is SPIRITUAL–SIN ENTERED. Since that terrible day, man has been involved in getting back into PROPER ORDER, so he can be pleasing to HIS GOD.

In Hebrews 11, we are given a grand photo of DIVINE ORDER and it would benefit all of us to study and adjust accordingly. Abel is listed first as a WORSHIPPER, experiencing PEACE WITH GOD from his offering and his worship. Next we have ENOCH who WALKED with God: too many today are trying to WALK with God and have not yet made peace with Him, or become REAL WORSHIPPERS FIRST. Next we have NOAH who, through his obedience, built the ark and became a WITNESS for God unto the world.

THE PICTURE IS POWERFUL. We cannot be a real WITNESS for God until we first WALK with Him. We cannot WALK with God unless we first come to an AGREEMENT, for how shall two walk together except they agreed? We cannot WALK with Him unless we have PEACE with Him which comes from our WORSHIP OF HIM in the area of ACCEPTABLE BLOOD SACRIFICE. Reversing the order makes the picture quite plain; we must first REPENT, ACCEPT CALVARY, and have PEACE WITH GOD–then WALK WITH GOD by AGREEING and SUBMITTING. Then we can be a WITNESS, DOING AS TOLD. Are you in ORDER?

KNOWING THE TIME, OUR GREATEST NEED

How often have we been stopped by someone who would ask, "HAVE YOU GOT THE TIME?" which was an indicator that the person who asked was moving through that moment totally blind to and unaware of THE TIME. I wonder if we as HIS PEOPLE are even aware about WHAT TIME IT REALLY IS SPIRITUALLY?

As I listen to various broadcasts, read articles and compare all these with the WORD OF GOD, I am made to know we are surely living in the LAST TIMES OF THE LAST DAYS. I have been praying for ISRAEL and that terrible situation, for our nation and MR. BUSH and all he must deal with, but above all, for the CHURCH in our city to become awake and on our tiptoes. God has visited our services wonderfully, but we, I think, are somewhat sleepy about our NEED TO GATHER THE HARVEST. Sometimes I feel like NOAH as he prepared for the IMPENDING DOOM AND WRATH OF GOD and for his own SALVATION VIA THE ARK.

I am watching many in this church acting like nothing big is going on, that they do not need to make some great changes regarding involvement and dedication. I fear that many here have become so INSULATED and quite INDIFFERENT regarding personal responsibility to GOD AND THE LOST. We have the CURE FOR THE WORST DISEASE, SIN, and seemingly many are keeping their mouths shut, wallets sealed and laughing their way into ETERNITY. I have noticed that many of you are finding it very easy to MISS SERVICES, DOING STUFF that does not HONOR GOD and simply just FLOATING AROUND as if JESUS WAS NOT REALLY COMING SOON. This is very SCARY to say the least for HE has told us what the various conditions would be like just before HIS RETURN.

May God grant us MERCY and a great SHAKING so we will not be found SLEEPING SPIRITUALLY in these DAYS OF HARVEST, WE must be about HIS BUSINESS NOW...

THE KEY TO THE IMPOSSIBLE— LOOK AT GOD

I have been teaching quite a bit of late regarding FAITH and all that it can do. I think I need to show clearly that the real issue with FAITH is not just gritting teeth and repeating, "I BELIEVE GOD, I BELIEVE GOD." I am not very persuaded with various types of lessons I have read and heard about how we are supposed to act after FAITH has been released. I feel we are complicating the issue; TRUSTING GOD TO TELL THE TRUTH AND TO DO AS HE HAS PROMISED should be very simple.

I think we need to LOOK AT WHO HAS PROMISED and then we will find it much easier to ask for whatever petition we desire. I do not think JESUS ever intended for MIRACLES, WONDERS, or ANSWERS TO VARIOUS PRAYERS to be some types of hard, tough things to acquire that only a few GIFTED FOLKS are really able to experience. "THESE SIGNS SHALL FOLLOW THEM THAT BELIEVE." It seems to me that OUR GREAT LORD meant that PROMISE to be for ANY AND ALL WHO BELIEVE. I feel most of us really do believe, but we also fight against DOUBTS AND QUESTIONS that seem to either STEAL OR SHAKE OUR EFFORTS. Jesus said, "IF YOU BELIEVE AND DOUBT NOT," which seems to say, BELIEVING IS SIMPLE, but often there are DOUBTS that challenge OUR BELIEVING.

I know from experience, many CHRISTIAN FOLKS do not EXPECT miracles or ANSWERS to prayers especially if something is being asked that has been accepted and lived with as normal. I have a great desire to somehow BREAK THROUGH the FAITH BARRIERS in my own life and finally TASTE VICTORY over SICKNESS, DISEASE AND DEVILS. I cannot accept the position often taken by many; this, that, or the other is just part of life and we have to make the best of it, NO! JESUS confronted and altered situations and sickness every time and so DID HIS FIRST CHURCH. WE MUST EARNESTLY CONTEND FOR THE FAITH THAT WAS ONCE DELIVERED TO THE SAINTS, for that is what impacted their world and brought HONOR TO GOD, nothing else will do. I'm reaching...

LET EVERY MAN EXAMINE HIMSELF

Paul wrote the above words to the church to challenge them to the very important work of SELF INSPECTION, so that they would not be SELF DECEIVED, OR SATAN DECEIVED, OR WORLD-VIEW DECEIVED. It seems to me that folks who attend various church services, work in some capacity or believe some dogmas, are very easily the best targets for the WORK OF DECEPTION. It seems we who are trying to do the work of the church, of seeking to save the lost, of spending our time involved with RELIGIOUS WORKINGS, CAN BE LACKING PERSONAL INSPECTIONS.

I know the BOOK shouts to all of us, "THE HEART IS DECEITFUL ABOVE EVERYTHING THAT IS FULL OF WICKED WAYS," and none of us really know what is within us. God has taken to HIMSELF that prerogative and we need to constantly go to HIM in prayer and ask for cleansing and purifying of OUR INNER MOTIVES AND AGENDAS. It seems to be so easy to LIE TO OURSELVES, OR TO BE VERY LENIENT WITH WEAK AREAS and so we must REALLY EXAMINE OURSELVES and try to walk IN HOLINESS AND PURITY. Paul knew how easy it was to be SELF DECEIVED by listing various things done, or not done, but that type of measuring leaves so much UNCHECKED.

We need to EXAMINE our PRAYER LIVES, not just that we pray and often, but are we getting INTO THE PRESENCE OF GOD and being impacted by it? Do we BREAK DOWN OR OPEN in our praying so that TEARS come flowing down on our cheeks? I wonder how long it has been for some since BROKENNESS AND WEEPING has happened? Do you pray with PASSION, or just with your PETITIONS? Have you made any progress in various areas of WEAKNESS, or just give up and go on? Has your LOVE FOR JESUS cooled so HE IS NOT A PRIORITY any longer, and how about CHURCH–no big deal to miss anymore?

Let all who read please EXAMINE YOURSELVES.

THE TRUTH LIBERATES AND CAN BE PROVEN

Jesus told us that the TRUTH MAKES FREE, and all through the Gospels, various claims made by MEN OR ANGELS were VALIDATED. I was reading in Luke 24:11 which states THEIR WORDS SEEMED LIKE IDLE TALES, they would not believe them. How often are people confronted with the LOVING AND WONDERFUL JESUS who has promised total PARDON, MERCY AND A FRESH START to any and all, yet many turn away in unbelief? It just seems too good to be true, or some may feel what they have heard is TRUE, but doesn't apply to them.

When I first heard of how the LORD JESUS wanted me to come to HIM, that HE wanted me AS HIS VERY OWN, I, too, seemed to be taken back and YET THAT VERY OFFER HAS BEEN PROVEN TRUE BY ME. He did forgive, he did ADOPT ME INTO HIS FAMILY, He did fill me with THE HOLY GHOST and He has been so wonderful to me. I want to go on RECORD; HIS TRUTH AND WORDS CAN BE PROVEN AND VALIDATED to anyone who would make an appeal in HIS DIRECTION. I continued to read the verses following and in 24 it shouts, "THEY FOUND IT EVEN SO!" The truths expounded, that had been disregarded, now had been VALIDATED, sometimes it takes some effort on our part to PROVE AND EXPERIENCE the very promises made unto us.

I am so glad that we serve A FAITHFUL CREATOR AND LOVING GOD who has HIMSELF gone on record often with words such as: PROVE ME NOW, MY WORD SHALL NOT RETURN UNTO ME VOID, KEEPING MY PROMISES TO THOUSANDS OF GENERATIONS, and on and on. Seems to me that God wants to be BELIEVED and takes it very personal when ANY PERSON challenges the very INTEGRITY AND POWER OF HIS WORDS. I want to believe and behave accordingly, I want to TESTI-

FY to all of you; TRUTH CAN BE PROVEN. While it may seem sometimes that a certain promise or premise SOUNDS LIKE AN IDLE TALE it is not A TALE, BUT HIS TRUTH and HE WILL BACK HIS WORD UP WITH A DEMONSTRATION if we will but ACT UPON IT IN FAITH.

Surely all of us delight to be BELIEVED when we share something that may seem OUTLANDISH OR IMPOSSIBLE. And yet how much more DOES GOD WANT US TO ACCEPT THE TRUTH and testify that it was found EVEN SO...

THE HIGHEST AIM OF OUR LIVES

So many of our ways are lived very contrary to what God wishes for us, simply THAT HE WOULD BE GLORIFIED IN OUR LIVES. To live with that idea in our minds would surely give us room for growth and for purified desires and actions. I really do want GOD to be GLORIFIED in everything I do, or even attempt. This concept will, of course, make us willing to be BURIED UNDER—as some seeds are that the HARVEST be obtained from that BURYING—and would bring HIM GLORY.

If we could adapt the idea that HIS BEING GLORIFIED is really the MAIN ISSUE, I think we could really be SET FREE from quite a lot of FRUSTRATIONS AND ANXIETY. To know that HE would choose our ways, our stops and our situations, we would be at REST knowing THIS WILL FIND ITS END BY GOD BEING GLORIFIED. That must have been how the 3 Hebrew boys surely felt when they stood against the call to bow to an IDOL. The punishment had been told to all, yet they seemed to say, IF OUR BURNING WILL BE TO HIS GLORY, get the furnace ready for we know THAT BOWING TO THAT DUMB IDOL WILL NOT GLORIFY OUR GOD.

We must grasp the truth that God often puts us into situations not so we can SHOWCASE OUR ABILITY, but rather that we can BEST BRING HIM GLORY. We may even be told to sit on the sidelines for a while so the GLORY will be HIS, and we will not be posing for pictures. I know that God let ELIJAH be somewhat sidelined from PUBLIC MINISTRY while ravens fed and a little drying brook slacked his thirst. I am sure it was quite a strain on him and then to be sent to a WIDOW, who was a heathen so he could be fed, surely was a blow to his EGO. From all this, God would be GLORIFIED IN HIM AND THROUGH HIM so the END WOULD SURELY JUSTIFY THE MEANS TO IT. May we also BRING HIM GLORY AND HONOR…

BE NOT WEARY IN WELL-DOING

It comes as no shock to many of us that Paul would admonish the CHURCH FOLKS to not be weary or faint while doing THE WORK OF GOD. I know that His work is the greatest, the best and finest, and yet it would be, and is, the most RESISTED, CONTESTED, AND AT TIMES, DISCOURAGING.

We have been invited to be a part of something that entails the ETERNAL WELL-BEING OF SOULS and the RESISTANCE of the EVIL AND SINISTER ONE. Remember, JESUS was forced to contend with him at various stages of MINISTRY, but never did HE CONCEDE DEFEAT OR QUIT. Come to think of it, we cannot QUIT, TURN AROUND AND JUST GIVE UP. The world needs our efforts even though they do not usually APPRECIATE our actions or attitudes. Remember, we have not been called to raise up a FOLLOWING, we have been commissioned to tell THE STORY OF JESUS, HIS GREAT LOVE, THE CROSS, PENTECOST AND THE COMING OF THE LORD.

It seems so easy to lose SIGHT OR HEART at times, but our work is TOO GREAT and the consequences are TOO HORRIBLE for us to just QUIT. Anyone can begin some type of PROJECT, but usually the excitement wears thin quickly and inspiration fades, but the UNFINISHED TASK shouts, "HEY YOU! FINISH WHAT YOU BEGAN!" Diets are started, a lot never finish, many attend elementary school, but few finish college, lots of cub scouts, but very few eagle scouts. The last time I checked, the REWARDS still show up at the finish line. Over and over the message screams from the HOLY PAGES, "HE THAT OVERCOMES!" "ENDURE TO THE END!" "HOLD FAST!" Jesus calls to all of us to continue, and uses HIMSELF as an EXAMPLE saying, "EVEN AS I ALSO OVERCAME..."

It was no picnic for JESUS; his days were long, filled with hurts, misunderstandings, hatred, resistance, faltering followers, forsaken by multitudes and finally, THE CROSS. The hill of suffering was the place that HE CRIED, "IT IS FINISHED." TIRED PREACHER, WEARY PARENT, MUCH DISCOURAGED PILGRIM–take heart and remember who it is THAT CALLED YOU; so FINISH YOUR JOB.

NOW UNTO HIM WHO IS ABLE TO EXCEED ANYTIME

The Great God we serve is totally awesome to say the least, in fact we cannot even start to imagine WHAT HE CAN AND WANTS TO DO FOR US. God has gone on record in the Bible with all types of stories under various obstacles and has always come through. I wonder if we even grasp HOW GREAT OUR GOD REALLY IS? He has never LIED, FAILED, MADE A MISTAKE, FORGOTTEN ANYONE, BEEN DEFEATED BY THE DEVIL, DISEASED, HAD FALSE DOCTRINES, EXPERIENCED MEMORY LOSS (EXCEPT ABOUT OUR FAILURES AND SINS), NOT KNOWN WHAT TO DO EVERY TIME, HAS NEVER BEEN SURPRISED BY ANY OF OUR ACTIONS, HE CAN MAKE ANYONE OVER ANEW, HAS MORE POWER AND ABILITY THAN CAN BE IMAGINED, IS FEARED AND REVERENCED BY HELL ITSELF AND ALL ITS HORDES, HAS NEVER MET ANY PERSON WHO HE COULD NOT HELP, FIX OR EVEN USE FOR HIS GLORY.

Sometimes, we need to pause a moment and study about HIS GREATNESS and the fact HE IS ON OUR SIDE ALL THE TIME. Calvary was for our BENEFIT, but also for HIS NAME to be honored for being so gracious and long-suffering. He showed HIS WISDOM through that sacrifice and great love for mankind. He has thus remained JUST AND JUSTIFIER for all who would accept HIS GREAT WORK AT THE CROSS. I am so glad HE is way beyond the average concept of HIM now being written about and spoken about in this time. He so far EXCEEDS every effort to try and explain, that I am boggled by HIS GREATNESS. Nothing can stop his purpose from happening–from the CHURCH being built to accomplishing the FINAL WORK ordained by HIM. No devil or doubter can circumvent the FULLNESS OF GOD now beginning to flow into our lives; the best is yet to happen.

God is not LIMITED to the past; HE can repeat anything needed, but consider what lies ahead: HE alone has the ability to EXCEED HIMSELF in every way that HE desires to and we are blessed to be a part of that grand operation. Thank God for ACTS, but I am looking ahead to HIS FINAL DEMONSTRATION in us just before the CHURCH LEAVES, it is NOT TOO GOOD TO BE TRUE, HE WILL MANIFEST HIMSELF shortly.

OUR WORLD IS CONFUSED, OUR GOD IS NOT

Daily I meet folks or hear some talking about various subjects and I am made aware HOW TOTALLY CONFUSED THIS WORLD IS about so many things, it is TRAGIC. I know many church folks (so called) only accept some portions of scripture as needful and vital for their lives today and some just kind–of HUNT AND PECK, PICK AND CHOOSE. I am so amazed at the GAUL AND FEARLESS ATTITUDE taken by many that THE WORD OF GOD is not really any big deal and that GOD seems to be the ONE THAT IS REALLY CONFUSED, or that HIS TEACHINGS are not RELEVANT for today. I want to go on record; GOD IS NOT IN ANY WAY MIXED UP, CONFUSED ABOUT RIGHT OR WRONG, THE WAGES OF SIN, THE LOCATION OF THE LAKE OF FIRE, ACTIVITIES UNACCEPTABLE TO HIM, THE PRICE REQUIRED TO SAVE THE LOST, HOW HE WILL JUDGE ALL FOLKS WHO REFUSE TO BE OBEDIENT WITH THE GOSPEL, OR THE STANDARD HE WILL USE ABOUT THE CHURCH BEING DEALT WITH.

In the garden, Satan challenged what God had told the couple–as if to insinuate that either God was hiding something they needed, or that they had just misunderstood what had been stated. Confusion seemed to be the issue then and seems to be the issue now. IS GOD CONFUSED ABOUT RIGHT AND WRONG? Is there really such a thing as ABSOLUTE? Am I to BELIEVE HIS WORD or just figure out for myself, WHAT HE IS MIXED UP ABOUT? I know this seems somewhat strange to ask, whether God is CONFUSED, but the people I have been dealing with seem to think HE REALLY WAS AND STILL IS.

I am so glad GOD IS RIGHT ABOUT ALL HE HAS TOLD US: HE IS THE ALL–WISE GOD WHO IS SO PERFECT, LIES ARE IMPOSSIBLE

AND SO IS FAILURE. Sometimes, what I am told to believe goes upstream and against the accepted norms of today, but so what! I am glad we have a GOD we can go to when we are perplexed and can get some help. I am so glad HE REIGNS TODAY IN SPITE OF ANY FOLKS OR SITUATIONS THAT MAY SAY HE DOES NOT. HE IS NOT CONFUSED, folks are...

GOD'S TWO REQUIREMENTS: BORN AGAIN, HOLINESS

Most churches today would probably say they believed the NEW BIRTH but of course they would begin to do away with any type of SUPERNATURAL EXPERIENCE such as occurred in ACTS. Most of this church would say they believed that unless we were BORN AGAIN like the BIBLE records we, like JESUS SAID, could not see nor enter HIS KINGDOM. I would like to go on record; TO BE HALF RIGHT IS TO BE HALF WRONG, MAKING US WRONG. We surely must be BORN AGAIN, but after that great event we are COMMANDED TO PURSUE HOLINESS; For without HOLINESS NO MAN SHALL SEE THE LORD. Now the crowd, even in this assembly, will start to either THIN OUT or come out EXPLAINING their personal slant on WHAT HOLINESS IS OR IS NOT.

Our church world is full of talk about GIFTS, LOVE, GROWTH, POWER, SIGNS; but one never hears any person saying, I WANT TO BE HOLY, I WANT TO BE LIKE GOD, I WANT TO GET AS CLOSE TO GOD AS I CAN. If anyone begins to talk about being HOLY, THEY ARE LOOKED AT AS WEIRD, STRANGE OR NOT IN THE REAL WORLD. Ask yourself now, do you want to be HOLY, are you really seeking to be LIKE HIM, are you yearning to lay aside anything that could be HINDERING HOLINESS in your life? I know I yearn to experience the POWER OF GOD within my own life in a greater measure but I am being made to see that POWER FLOWS FROM A PURITY within our beings. God will not flow in and out of a person in any degree while that person plays with UNHOLY THINGS, ENJOYS UNHOLY DESIRES, WILLFULLY WALKS IN UNHOLY WAYS; it just cannot be done. YE THAT LOVE THE LORD, HATE EVIL, EVERY EVIL WAY, ANYTHING THAT HINDERS FROM BEING HOLY. The book tells the SAINTS, to clear ourselves from all the filthiness of THE FLESH AND SPIRIT, PERFECTING HOLINESS IN THE FEAR OF GOD. We are also told to GLORIFY GOD IN OUR BODIES AND SPIRITS, FOR WE ARE NOT OUR OWN, WE HAVE BEEN BOUGHT WITH A PRICE.

Are you HOLY in WORDS, DEEDS, AND LEISURE TIMES; seeking to WALK THE WAY OF THE HOLY. May God grant to all of us A FRESH FIRE to pursue HOLINESS, for without it WE WILL NEVER SEE THE LORD. Help us LORD JESUS.

THE VALUE OF GOOD INSTRUMENTS

The carpenter relies upon his tools to be correct for whatever job is being done and also that his saw is sharp and the proper cutting type. No real builder of various items would even think about doing quality work without the best of tools to aid his efforts. Consider what type of music would come to the ear if the wrong instruments were played for certain parts, or worse; the instruments were out of tune or broken down. Guitars missing strings, a drum with a hole in the skin, violins with loose strings, a trumpet clogged, and so on. Without the instrument being correct and in good shape, the person working or playing could not be able to perform at PEAK.

Now consider the same truth with regards to GOD AND HIS SAVED VESSELS. We are the INSTRUMENTS that GOD plays upon, works through and if we are in terrible condition, or out of tune with HIS PURPOSES, what can we ever accomplish for HIM? It is needful that we are careful to keep ourselves in SPIRITUAL CONDITION so that GOD WILL BE HONORED as we render the BEST SERVICE NEEDED. Tools are such necessary items to function within certain job arenas. Shall not we take care about the condition of our own being with regard to BEING USED IN THE ARENA OF SOULS. Often times I have had to replace various tools because of bad shape, or broken or just not proper for my needs. I have also had to take my wood saw and have it sharpened after I had worked myself half to death over a dull edge. May God help each of us to be in the condition we ought to be so that God will be pleased with our performance and impact for HIS GLORY will occur...

YOU MAY ORDER MORE COPIES OF THIS SERIES BY CONTACTING:

The Pentecostals of Gainesville
Attn: Truth Publications
8105 NW 23rd Avenue
Gainesville, FL 32606
352.376.6320

Please send check or money order to the address above or see our web site listed below.

There will be future books of this series.

Look for these books and more by Reverend J.W. Arnold:

The Why and Wonder of Worship Volume I
The Why and Wonder of Worship Volume II
The Why and Wonder of Worship Volume III
Five More Minutes

Web Site:
www.gainesvilleupc.net